D1636871

THE GENIUS
OF THE WEST

Louis Rougier

THE GENIUS
OF THE WEST

with an Introduction by F. A. v. Hayek

Nash Publishing, Los Angeles

Library of Congress Catalog Card Number: 76-93466
Standard Book Number: 8402-5001-0

Published simultaneously in the United States and Canada
by Nash Publishing Corporation, 9255 Sunset Boulevard,
Los Angeles, California 90069.

Printed in the United States of America

First printing

This volume is a publication of
The Principles of Freedom Committee

The great body of economic and political literature since World War II—both academic and popular—has presented a misleading picture of the performance of private enterprise and of the State in the economies of the free world. This literature exaggerates the defects of the one and the merits of the other. Freedom will remain in jeopardy unless the public gains a clearer picture of the workings of the free market and comes to realize that its greatest virtue is not its extraordinary capacity to produce widely diffused material benefits, important as this merit is, but its unique capacity to protect the great immaterial values of our Western Heritage.

As a means of increasing the flow of literature that would correct the picture and strengthen the foundations of freedom, a group calling itself the Principles of Freedom Committee was formed during the early 1960's to promote a series of books dealing with important economic and political issues of the day. To assist in the international publication and distribution of the books, the Committee recruited an advisory group of scholars from sixteen countries. *The Genius of the West* is the fourth book in the Principles of Freedom Series.

The membership of the Committee has changed over the years through retirements and replacements by cooption. The original members were Professors Milton Friedman (University of Chicago), F. A. Hayek, G. Warren Nutter, B. A. Rogge, and John V. Van Sickle. Executive Secretary; Ruth Sheldon Knowles, Project Coordinator; and Byron K. Trippet, Committee Member Ex-Officio. Dr. Trippet retired in 1965 following his resignation as President of Wabash College. Professors Hayek and Nutter retired in 1968, and three new members were added: Gottfried Haberler, Galen L. Stone Professor of International Trade, Harvard University; F. A. Harper, President, Institute for Humane Studies; and Don Paarlberg, Hillenbrand Professor of Agricultural Economics, Purdue University. In 1970 Gottfried Dietze, Professor of Political Science at The Johns Hopkins University, joined the Committee.

The original Committee requested modest nonrecurring grants from a number of corporations and foundations. These donors receive copies of all books as they appear, and their help in promoting the distribution of the books is welcomed. The Institute for Humane Studies handles the funds received from the project's supporters and issues annual reports. Decisions as to authors, subjects, and acceptability of manuscripts rest exclusively with the Committee.

Volumes in the Principles of Freedom Series are:

> *Great Myths of Economics* (1968) by Don Paarlberg
>
> *The Strange World of Ivan Ivanov* (1969) by G. Warren Nutter
>
> *Freedom in Jeopardy: The Tyranny of Idealism* (1969) by John V. Van Sickle
>
> *The Regulated Consumer* (1971) by Mary Bennett Peterson

à John V. Van Sickle
à l'initiative duquel
je dois d'avoir écrit ce livre,
avec toute mon affectueuse gratitude

Louis Rougier

CONTENTS

Introduction   xv

I. GREEK RATIONALISM:
    THE BEGINNINGS OF THEORETICAL SCIENCE   1
    The Promethean Myth
    The Development of Rational Thought:
        the Creation of Logic
    The Creation of Axiomatic and Deductive Geometry
    The Demythologizing of Nature
    The Creation of Mathematical Physics
    The Creation of Scientific Geography
    The Science of Aesthetics and the
        Theory of Propositions

II. GREEK RATIONALISM: DEMOCRACY, A MONEY
    ECONOMY AND THE SCIENCE OF ETHICS   13
    Democracy and the Rule of Law
    A Money Economy
    Ethics as a Science
    Writing and the Democratization of Greek Culture
    Freedom of Thought and the Absence of
        Religious Dogmatism
    The Balance Sheet of Hellenism

[ix]

III. ROMAN ORDER   26
     Roman Law
     Roman Universalism
     The *Pax Romana*

IV. THE HANDICAP OF ANCIENT CIVILIZATIONS:
     SLAVERY   33
     Why the Scientific Knowledge of the Greeks
        Did Not Lead to an Industrial Revolution
     Slavery Discredited the Mechanical Arts
     Aristotle's Justification of Slavery
     The Decline of the Scientific Spirit
     The Revenge of Spartacus

V. THE SOCIAL REVOLUTION OF CHRISTIANITY   44
     The Moral Rehabilitation of the Slave
     The Rehabilitation of Manual Labor and the
        Mechanical Arts
     Inventions in the Middle Ages
     How the Development of Medieval Technology
        Encouraged Scientific Research

VI. THE RENAISSANCE   56
     The New Humanism
     The Rediscovery of Ancient Greece
     Plato in Florence
     The Universal Man
     The Golden Age of the Medici
     The Spread of the Renaissance
     The Secularization of Life
     The Great Discoveries

VII. THE SCIENTIFIC REVOLUTION   65
     The Rediscovery of the Scientific Works of Antiquity
     The Reawakening of the Scientific Spirit
        and the Insistence that It Be Useful
     The Giants of the Renaissance:
        Leonardo da Vinci
        Francis Bacon

Galileo Galilei
René Descartes
The Age of Academies Begins

VIII. THE CONFLICT BETWEEN THEOLOGY
       AND SCIENCE   74
       The Conflict between the Bible and the
          Scientific Spirit
       The Conflict between Aristotle and the
          Scientific Spirit
       The Four Criteria of Truth
       The Incompatibility between Scripture,
          Aristotle and the Copernican System
       The Letter of Galileo to the
          Grand Duchess of Tuscany
       The Trial of Galileo
       The Secularization of Science

IX. THE NEW IMAGE OF THE WORLD AND THE
     IDEA OF PROGRESS   87
     The Closed World of Aristotle
     The Open World of Galileo
     The Idea of Progress
     Turgot, Buffon and Condorcet
     The Philosophy of History

X. THE PROTESTANT ETHIC AND THE APPEARANCE
    OF THE CAPITALIST MENTALITY   95
    The Economy of the Ancient World
    The Moral Economy of the Middle Ages
    Calvinism: A Turning Point
    The Protestant Ethic and Modern Capitalism
    The Secularization of the Protestant Ethic

XI. THE ECONOMIC REVOLUTION   106
     Economics in Antiquity and the Middle Ages
     Mercantilism and Economic Warfare
     Free Trade and Peace

The French Physiocrats
Adam Smith and the Market Economy

XII. THE INDUSTRIAL REVOLUTION   117
The First Phase
The Second Phase
The Agricultural Revolution
The Cybernetics Revolution

XIII. THE POLITICAL REVOLUTION   126
Christianity and the Distinction between the
    Temporal and the Spiritual
Mixed Governments and the Balance of Power
The Beginning of Parliaments:
The Historic Rights of the Englishman
From the Historic Rights of Englishmen to the
    Natural Rights of Man
The French Revolution
The Liberal Conception of the State

XIV. THE ACHIEVEMENT OF FREEDOM OF THOUGHT   142
Religious Tolerance in Antiquity
Christianity and Religious Intolerance
The Struggles for Tolerance and the
    Neutrality of the State
The Achievement of Freedom of
    Speech and of the Press

XV. THE TAKE-OFF OF THE WEST   155
The Abolition of the Corporations
The Rise of the Proletariat as a Protest against the
    Market Economy
The Marxian Answer to the Challenge Presented by
    the Proletarian Condition
Modern Capitalism's Answer to the Challenge
    Presented by the Proletarian Condition
The Transformation of the World by the
    Market Economy

XVI. WESTERN CIVILIZATION AND THE CIVILIZATIONS
OF THE EAST   170

The Incompatibility of Traditional Chinese
Mentality with the Idea of Progress
The Incompatibility of the Traditional Hindu
Mentality with the Idea of Progress
How Arab Civilization Was Fettered by Islam

XVII. THE RISKS OF PROGRESS   181

The Eighteenth Century's Belief in
Continuous Progress
How Progress Draws from Itself New Challenges
The Population Explosion
The Nuclear Explosion
The Welfare State
Progress: The Child of Challenge

XVIII. CONCLUSION   192

Notes   201

Index   217

INTRODUCTION

by

F. A. v. Hayek

This is a book which has long been needed. In remarkably short compass it gives us a brilliant survey of the development over a span of more than two thousand years of those ideas which have shaped the political order and indeed the civilization of the West. Few scholars possess the encyclopedic knowledge needed to write such a book and fewer still the skill to tell the story in a form attractive to the general reader. Professor Rougier is that rare exception, a scholar and a writer.

Until a few generations ago most educated people had some concept of the origin and growth of the ideas and conceptions that have shaped this civilization. Consequently some sort of common view prevailed which, though often distorted and naively idealized, provided a basis of communication. But this is no longer true, in part because of the progressive elimination of the "classics" from the education of the young, and in part because the rapid increase in our knowledge of the past has somewhat discredited the standard picture once so generally taught in the schools. Popular accounts of the results of recent specialized research abound, but to my knowledge Professor Rougier has provided the thoughtful reader with the first satisfying overall statement of the growth of those conceptions which have led to the formation of the free societies of the West.

The author brings unique qualifications to this task. A distinguished philosopher with a lifelong interest in the history of philosophy and science, he has for more than thirty years devoted increasing attention to the contemporary political scene. Indeed, at one stage he did much to start the movement for the revival of the basic principles of a free society which is now one of the hopeful signs of our times. In 1938, shortly after the publication of Walter Lippmann's remarkable *Inquiry into the Principles of the Good Society* (Boston: Little, Brown and Company, 1937), he convened in Paris a gathering of scholars who shared Lippmann's concern about the new threats to personal liberty and who, after a fascinating discussion, agreed to form a *Centre Internationale des Études pour la Renovation du Liberalism*—this at a time when the term "liberal" had not yet been appropriated by the opponents of liberty. But when the report of this meeting appeared in print (*Colloque Walter Lippmann,* Paris, 1939), only a few weeks were left before the outbreak of the Second World War and the consequent suspension of all efforts of this nature. The efforts, however, were revived immediately after the war, and it was around the group Professor Rougier had brought together that a larger international association of friends of personal liberty was formed.

During the war Professor Rougier returned to problems in the area of pure philosophy. In 1955 he published his great *Traite de la Connaissance,* followed five years later by his *Metaphysique et le Langage.* But his continuing concern at the direction political developments in the West were taking found expression soon thereafter in his profound analysis of the weaknesses of French democracy (*L'Erreur de la Democratie Francaise,* 1962). It was in this period also that he published his brilliant article, "Valeur et Avenir de la Civilisation Occidentale" (*La Revue des deux Mondes,* October 1, 1958), out of which the present book has grown. Appreciating the significance of this article and its relevance to the objectives they were seeking to promote, the Committee sponsoring this Series urged Professor Rougier to expand the theme of the article into a book. He agreed, and the result has more than fulfilled the Committee's expectations.

Even in translation and with the cutting needed to fit the manuscript into the format of the Principles of Freedom Series, the reader will find the book at once profound and eloquent, and studded with passages that are invitations to long reflection. The argument is easy to follow. The book is that rare combination of scholarly solidity and good writing that one finds more often in French than in any other literature. Despite the universality of the theme, *The Genius of the West* remains distinctly French. To Professor Rougier the ideas that have produced our Western civilization, ideas which he has traced back in masterly fashion to their beginnings in antiquity and the Middle Ages, essentially culminate in the rationalism of the eighteenth century, and above all in that of the French Enlightenment. This view is widely held outside as well as within France. To me, to be fully acceptable this high praise given to the achievements of the thinkers of the Enlightenment requires that a distinction be drawn between different views of rationalism—and perhaps even the admission that some of Rougier's *philosophes* carried their rationalism too far. And indeed Rougier has recognized this, as can be seen in his acute discussion of the limits of rationalism in *Le Paralogism du Rationalism* (1920), an early work which established his scholarly reputation.

Specialists will inevitably find matters to criticize in a book which ventures into so many fields. Some economists will doubtless question Professor Rougier's interpretation of modern economic history, as in the role he assigns to Henry Ford. But these, and other minor points of disagreement I might make, in nowise detract from my admiration for Professor Rougier's achievement nor lessen my conviction that he has provided a valuable starting point for all those concerned with understanding and preserving Western civilization.

While Rougier stresses the importance of the lessons we can learn from a study of the past, he does not claim that the wisdom of the past is all we need to solve the problems of the future. All he is saying, and it is all that reasonable men can say, is that we are not likely to handle successfully the problems that face us if we do not understand and build upon the ideas which have shaped our civilization.

Some readers may feel, mistakenly, I believe, that Professor Rougier is unduly optimistic concerning the powers of human reason. Nobody could be more aware than he how fragile Western civilization is, and how grave the danger that intellectual error may destroy it. He does believe, however, that problems do not solve themselves—that the use of intelligence is important. Yet precisely because of our confidence in the power of reason it is perhaps more important than ever before that we become fully aware of the role ideals have played in the formation of this civilization which is now so gravely threatened.

The ideals on which the present American society rests have their roots deep in Europe's history. Americans will not only not understand that old continent, they will not even understand themselves, unless they know that history. And what is true for the Americans is even truer for the peoples of the younger nations.

It took a lifetime of effort for men of my generation to achieve even a dim and fragmentary picture of this civilization. I almost envy the young of today. They will find it vastly easier to capture the picture in its fascinating entirety because they can start their voyage into the past with the clear and coherent account that Professor Rougier has provided in *The Genius of the West.*

I

GREEK RATIONALISM:
THE BEGINNINGS OF
THEORETICAL SCIENCE

THE PROMETHEAN MYTH

According to Arnold Toynbee, a civilization always rests on some basic myth. The myth undergirding the civilization of the West is the myth of Prometheus.

Prometheus was the philanthropic hero who dared defy the will of Zeus by stealing fire from heaven and giving it to mortal men whom that jealous "tyrant of the heavens and the earth" had decided to destroy.[1] The story prefigures the spirit of the West. It expresses the spirit of revolt against the prohibitions of jealous gods, which symbolize the fears of primitive peoples in the presence of natural forces which dominate and terrify them. It expresses the curiosity and love of adventure which drove Ulysses to unknown horizons and enabled him to overcome the perils of the seas through intelligence and courage. It embodies that love of action which incited Hercules to rid the earth of tyrants, brigands, and monsters, to tame the rivers and drain the swamps. It is that thirst for knowledge which led Pliny the Elder to risk his life by going to the very brink of Vesuvius in eruption. It is the critical spirit against superstition, celebrated by Lucretius in his praise of Epicurus: "When human life lay prostrate on the earth, visibly crushed down under the visage of a religion lowering menacingly from heaven over mortals, a man, a Greek, was the first who dared to lift his mortal eyes against her." [2]

Western civilization is a product of this attitude. Promethean implies a refusal to be satisfied with the human lot as it is, an insistence on the possibility of improving things and shaping them to fit man's needs and dreams.

THE DEVELOPMENT OF RATIONAL THOUGHT: THE CREATION OF LOGIC

This mentality did not originate with the Greeks, but they were the first to develop it systematically. The Greek contribution to Western civilization consisted in giving substance to the word "reason."

In contrast to the Oriental, who submitted himself in silence to the commands of the gods and the dictates of kings, the Greek tried to understand the world he lived in. He respected only such laws as he himself had a voice in shaping. In place of the soothsayers, prophets, seers, and astrologers of the East, we encounter among the Greeks an entirely new breed of men—dialecticians, sophists, philosophers and intellectuals who sought to persuade by the power of reason, by demonstrating the logical necessity of abstract relationships. In place of the empirical routine of Eastern thought, the Greeks substituted the science of proof.

This science is not satisfied with the evidence of the senses which describes the *how* of things; it insists upon intellectual evidence which can explain the *why*. In place of the practical geometry of the Egyptians we get the axiomatic and deductive geometry of the Pythagoreans; in place of the calculations of the Phoenician traders, the theory of numbers; in place of the descriptive and numeric astronomy of the Babylonians, the theoretical and explanatory astronomy of Eudoxus, Hipparchus and Ptolemy, which explains the apparently capricious movements of the planets by a geometric combination of simple, circular and uniform movements in an expanded universe.

In place of the theogonies of Homer and Hesiod, we find that first the Milesian philosophers and then the Atomists substituted the science of physics, which had as its goal the explanation of all phenomena, celestial as well as terrestrial, by means of purely natural causes. In place of the magical and priestly medicine of the East, Asclepiades and his followers developed a science of healing founded upon clinical observations. For the legendary tales of the bards there were substituted narrative history by Herodotus and interpretive history by Thucydides and Polybius. New words appear which have no equivalents in the ancient Oriental languages: theory, demonstration, logic, and syllogism. These register the "quantum leap" of the human spirit achieved by Greece. The Greeks discovered the power of deductive thinking, the rules of demonstration.

The Greeks of the Eleatic school had earlier distinguished the domain of *opinion* from the domain of *truth*. Opinion, they explained, rests on the fallible testimony of the senses, whereas truth is disclosed only to the intelligence. "The eyes and the ears are shabby witnesses," wrote Heraclitus, "if those who see and hear do not possess souls capable of interpreting language." [3] From the domain of opinion came the rhetoric which flourished on the lips of lawyers and political orators in the city-states. One learned this art for the purpose of mastering and directing the aimless thoughts of the crowd, making a doubtful opinion convincing. Filled with the newly discovered joy of arguing and reasoning, the Greeks frequently fell into the vice of arguing for its own sake, which leads to the pyrrhonism of the Skeptics and the pragmatism of the Cynics. The Sophists took delight in raising in the public squares contradictions such as the one about Epimenides from Crete who asserted that all Cretans are liars: Is Epimenides, a Cretan, lying or telling the truth?

The dialectic of Plato was concerned with the domain of truth and became in the hands of Aristotle the method of demonstrating the logical necessity of a proposition by starting with other propositions previously accepted by all disputants. It was for the purpose of refuting sophisms that Aristotle created logic—the rules of coherent thinking—an accomplishment which led the Middle Ages to regard him as "the father of thinking men."

Aristotle developed the logic of classes. The Stoics went further and developed the logic of propositions. The resulting rules of argument enabled the Greek scholars to expound their disciplines in the form of deductive theories based on axioms. Certain literary fragments enable us to trace back to Thales (ca. 600 B.C.) the creation of deductive geometry. But, according to Proclus, the credit for this marvelous tool of reasoning goes primarily to Pythagoras (582–ca. 507 B.C.) and his followers: "And then came Pythagoras who transformed geometry into an essential part of a liberal education, because he went back to first principles and from them developed demonstrations of theories in a manner that was at once abstract and rational." [4] Geometry was the favored of the four Pythagorean sciences—the others being arithmetic, astronomy and music—which the Greeks developed by deducing a train of consequences from a few original principles.

THE CREATION OF AXIOMATIC AND
DEDUCTIVE GEOMETRY

There were geometricians in Egypt, astronomers in Babylon, and accountants in Phoenicia before there were mathematicians in Greece. But what a difference. An Egyptian papyrus from the twelfth dynasty, written by Ahmose I, makes the distinction clear. From Ahmose we learn that Egyptian surveyors had observed that if a rope were passed around three stakes separated from one another by distances represented by the numbers 3, 4, and 5, the sections of the rope corresponding to the distances 3 and 4 were perpendicular to one another. Egyptian geometricians noted the fact but made no attempt to explain it. To Orientals, such relationships were to be wondered at just as they wondered at the earth, the sky, rivers, mountains, trees and flowers. Quite different was the reaction of the Greeks. They were not content simply to find such discoveries wonderful. They wanted to discover a rational explanation for such marvels by finding out why this and no other relationship was required for constructing a right angle. By reducing this relationship to other equivalents, they succeeded in demonstrating the Pythagorean theorem.[5]

The problems posed in Oriental mathematics received solutions in the form of practical precepts to be followed case by case, devoid of concern for underlying general principles. There were rules of action sufficient for a surveyor or an architect, rules which rested on examples only and never on general demonstrations. And often these rules were applied to cases where the fit was imperfect. Even if Ahmose knew how to figure the area of a square or a rectangle, his formula would not be sufficient for calculating the area of other four-sided figures.

Greek geometry was not limited to empiricism. By substituting rational evidence for that derived from the senses, it escaped the limitations imposed by special cases. In place of visible qualities capable of being traced on sand or wax tablets, the Greeks substituted quantitative relationships capable of being understood through an effort of the mind.

Rising from the concrete to the abstract, Greek geometry disengaged the intelligible essence from the particular observable details, or accidents, as such particulars were later to be called. In this it exercised the proper function of intelligence: the faculty of abstracting, of grasping the unity of a concept in a number of particular cases, the constancy of relationships and permanence of structures amid the diversity of sensible patterns; in a word, finding unity in multiplicity and harmony in discord. With the Greek language was born the language of abstraction.

The proper function of intelligence is to discover the logical entailment of propositions with the aid of the two methods identified by Plato: *analysis,* which consists in deducing from a given proposition a series of equivalent consequences until one arrives at a proposition admitted to be true or previously demonstrated; and *synthesis,* which consists in reversing the sequence. The Greeks raised mathematics to the dignity of a demonstrative science and then dissected the structure of deductive theory by distinguishing according to their logical functions axioms, postulates, lemmas, theorems, problems, and porisms.[6]

The axiomatic and deductive method seemed to have been carried to such a degree of perfection in Euclid that the expression *more geometrico* (in the fashion of geometry) became the synonym for demonstrative method. But the mathematical sciences seemed to be studying a world apart, one having a purely conceptual existence, an intelligible world of pure numbers and ideal figures. The second miracle of Greek reason was the discovery that one could apply mathematics to the study of nature, which permitted the creation of mathematical physics. To arrive at this point, the Greeks had to start by demythologizing nature.

THE DEMYTHOLOGIZING OF NATURE

The early Greeks, like the Orientals, sought to explain the world with the aid of myths, the oldest traces of which are to be found in the Homeric poems (ninth century B.C.) and especially in the *Theogony* of Hesiod (ca. 700 B.C.):

At first Chaos came to be, but next wide-flanked Earth . . . and Eros . . . From Chaos came Erebus and black Night, and of Night were born Aether and Day . . . and Earth first bore starry Heaven, equal to herself, to cover her on every side . . . And she brought forth the high hills . . . and Pontus the fruitless sea, without the aid of Eros. But afterwards she lay with Heaven and bore deep swirling Oceanus . . .[7]

Then followed the Titans, the Cyclops and the race of the gods.

The popular picture of the universe, to be distinguished from the picture given by bards and poets, was suggested by the witness of the senses: a hemispheric world consisting of a flat earth covered by a rounded vault over which the "fixed" stars and the so-called "wandering" stars (the sun, the moon, and the five planets known to the ancients) pursued their varied courses.[8]

This conception of the world rested upon the belief in the absolute value of the vertical above our heads, which permitted giving an absolute topological meaning to notions of height and depth. The universe was thought of as having three stories: the *celestial* world, comprised of everything between the orbit of the moon and the hemisphere of the fixed stars, where everything was incorruptible and divine; the *terrestrial* world where everything was changing, corruptible and mortal; and the *infernal* world of Hades, the shadowy realm of the dead, whose shades were invoked by Ulysses.

It was this compartmentalized world picture that the first Greek physicists abandoned in favor of an essentially monistic concept of the universe, devoid of mythology. Physics—the study of nature—was born on the shores of Ionia in the sixth century B.C. The three great thinkers, Thales, Anaximander and Anaximenes, who followed one another in Miletus, the richest city of Greek Asia, had double merit. They proclaimed a principle of invariance, expressed in the adage, "Nothing creates itself, nothing destroys itself; there is nothing but combination and separation of things which already exist." This became our modern principle of the conservation of energy in a closed system. In conformity with this adage the Greeks taught that the different kinds of bodies which populate the world, and their motions, result from differences in states of condensation and rarefaction of some primitive matter. They thus found themselves asserting the principle of the substantial unity of the world.

They also sought to explain by purely natural causes, conforming to the preceding principles, such phenomena as the production of meteors, the formation of stars, the origin of light, and the genesis of the world. "They say," wrote Plato, "that fire, water, earth and air are products of nature and of *chance* and that art has no part in it." [9] It was from these inanimate elements that the great bodies of the universe were thought to have taken shape: earth, sun, moon and stars. Tossed off by pure chance, they combined themselves by chance. Fortunate results were produced haphazardly amid countless defeats. Plato continued: "It is in this fashion that the sky was produced in its entirety with all the celestial bodies, all plant-life, all animals, the succession of the seasons, not owing to reason nor to any god or art but owing, as we have said, to nature and to chance." [10]

THE CREATION OF MATHEMATICAL PHYSICS

The Milesians and the Abderites created physics by demythologizing nature. The Pythagoreans went further. They and their successors created mathematical physics by their discovery that the universe has a structure which can be expressed in mathematical terms; that the phenomena which follow one another obey immutable quantitative laws; and that the world truly deserves to be called the cosmos, because in it all is order, number, weight, and measure. The work of Pythagoras proves this point, particularly his two theories of mathematical physics: acoustics and geometric astronomy.

A theory of mathematical physics proceeds like a deductive mathematical theory. It sets up a certain number of hypotheses from which it proves and deduces certain logical consequences. But it adds to the requirement of logical coherence a second requirement, known to the ancients as "saving the appearances"; that is to say, staying close to how things seem in the world of experience. Nothing illustrates better the distance between the empiricism of the East and the rationalism of the Greeks than a comparison of Babylonian and Hellenic astronomy.

The untiring watchtower observers of the Euphrates valley had noted the angular movements of the stars and had succeeded, by a miracle of patience, in representing these movements by a numerical series which enabled them to foresee the oppositions and conjunctions of different planets with the sun, their risings and settings, their passage near the stars, and their entry into different signs of the zodiac; in brief, everything that interested Oriental astronomy. But this numerical astronomy remained purely descriptive. The Babylonians never bothered about determining the respective distances of the stars, about measuring their orbits geometrically, about explaining their apparently capricious movements.

Pythagoras discovered that the lazy and wandering course of the sun across the heavens could be explained by combining two circular and uniform movements: one directed from the east to the west, traveling in one day around the poles of the celestial sphere: the other being directed from west to east, traveling in one year around its circle, the ecliptic, inclined on the equator of the celestial sphere. This discovery suggested the idea that the movements of the so-called wandering stars, the planets, are as regular as the daily movements of the fixed stars, that their wandering movements only seem capricious because of a simple optical illusion. The Pythagoreans and Plato then posed to the geometricians this problem: How do you reconcile the apparent movement of the stars wrongly called wandering by means of circular and uniform movements? Eudoxus of Cnidus, friend and disciple of Plato, furnished a first solution with this theory of concentric spheres, which, corrected by Callippus and incorporated by Aristotle into his system, dominated the thought of the Middle Ages.

To construct this theory, Greek astronomers had to go beyond the evidence of the senses and resort to abstract reasoning for the explanation.[11] As their observations, aided by improved instruments, became more precise, Greek astronomers, in their efforts to "save appearances," complicated their hypotheses by recourse to cycles and epicycles. Ptolemy in his *Mathematical Syntax* provided the synthesis of their knowledge. It is by the same method of mathematical deduction and experimental control that Euclid developed his optics and Archimedes his researches into the statics of solids and liquids. It was in the course of reading these works that Leonardo da Vinci, Tartaglia, and above all Galileo were to learn the art of applying mathematics to nature and would realize the scientific revolution which started Western civilization along the path of industry and technology.

THE CREATION OF SCIENTIFIC GEOGRAPHY

Greek astronomers were not content to explain the apparent movements of the stars on the basis of geometric hypotheses; they sought to measure the size of the earth and the distances which separate it from the planets and the fixed stars.

Pythagoras was apparently the first to maintain that the earth is round and that the vertical is relative to a given center. To the question, Is the earth round or flat? Socrates came out for roundness. Aristotle provides supporting arguments of both a logical and an experimental nature. But it was Eratosthenes, director of the Alexandrian Museum from 240 to 200 B.C., who produced the definitive proof by scientifically calculating the circumference of the globe, with an error of less than 1 percent.[12]

Nor did Greek astronomers stop with measuring the radius and the circumference of the earth. Believing it to be contained within a sphere, that of the fixed stars, they were eager to measure the dimensions of the universe. Aristarchus perfected two ingenious methods for accomplishing this, but the instruments at his disposal inevitably introduced errors into his observations. He estimated the diameter of the sun as six or seven times the distance of the moon from the earth, and he gave to the radius of the sphere of the fixed stars a value immensely great in relationship to the radius of the earth. Hipparchus of Alexandria, the greatest astronomer of antiquity, calculated the distance of the moon from the earth as 67 or 68 terrestrial radii and its diameter as one-third that of our globe. He placed the sun at approximately 13,000 terrestrial radii from the earth. It was thanks to these figures, inaccurate as they proved to be, that myth and fiction were chased from the sky. The earth little by little lost its rank as Mother Goddess. With the use of physical instruments and mathematical devices, the Greek spirit burst the limits of terrestrial space and, aided by the rigorous logic of geometry, launched itself upon the conquest of the heavens. The results served to establish the maps which would render the greatest service to navigators and merchants.

THE SCIENCE OF AESTHETICS AND THE
THEORY OF PROPOSITIONS

The Greek rationalism that created mathematical physics and natural sciences was also reflected in the realm of art. Greek art was not dominated by magic, as was the monumental and figurative art of the Egyptians, nor were the Greeks limited to the iridescence of colors. They held art subject to the science of numbers and the harmonies of an intelligible order. In the arrangement of a Greek temple can be seen the harmonious relationships and proportions which are the abstract skeleton of sensible beauty. Precisely as they quantified the universe, the Greeks quantified aesthetics. Their sculpture obeyed mathematical rules; their architecture had the same regulations; their cities were built to plan. Their music rested upon the arithmetic and geometric study of intervals and musical harmonies. Harmonic and symphonic conceptions echoed back from music into their architecture and plastic arts.[13] The Greeks discovered the mathematical laws of beauty exactly as they anticipated the quantitative laws of the cosmos.

II

GREEK RATIONALISM: DEMOCRACY, A MONEY ECONOMY AND THE SCIENCE OF ETHICS

DEMOCRACY AND THE RULE OF LAW

The revolution which the Greeks introduced into the sciences and the arts penetrated into their social relations as well. Athenian democracy is as much a product of Greek rationalism as is deductive geometry.

Democracy may be defined as government by law as opposed to government by men. Because they lived under the rule of law, the Greeks called themselves free men. In contrast to the Persians and the barbarians, the Greeks were not subject to the discretionary will of despots. The laws of Solon guaranteed civil liberty for the Greeks throughout their long history by forbidding the enslavement of insolvent debtors; the laws of Pericles guaranteed political equality by inaugurating payment for public services, which opened up to citizens of the most humble station all civil offices except those dealing with the city's safety. As far as the law was concerned, everyone was free to live as he saw fit. Here we have one of the truly great social innovations in the long history of human society.

To understand the importance of this innovation one only

has to read in Herodotus the debate among Darius, Otanes, and Megabazus regarding the relative merits of democracy, aristocracy, and monarchy. In arguing for democracy, Otanes condemns the way kings are accountable to no one and act as they see fit. This leads the monarch to blameworthy actions, the result in some cases of excessive pride and in others of envy. An oligarchic or aristocratic regime is one in which power is confined to a small class of wealthy people who exploit the masses.[1] Democracy, on the other hand, means equality before the law; it is a government for rich and poor alike. Aristotle, like Plato before him, declared that "democracy is founded on liberty," something that is only possible "where all are equal." [2]

The Greek conception of democracy finds admirable expression in the speech, which Thucydides attributes to Pericles, delivered at the tomb of the soldiers who had died in the Peloponnesian War:

Our government is called a democracy because its control is in the hands of the many, not of the few. All men are equal before the law in the settlement of their private disputes, and public honors are bestowed on a man according to his merit, not because he belongs to a particular class . . . No one is kept from public office because of poverty or obscure rank; all who can serve the state are expected to do so.[3]

The Greeks reserved the term *polis* for a city governed by law. From its appearance somewhere between the eighth and seventh centuries B.C., the rule of law as voted by the Assembly of the citizens modified all human relationships and created an entirely new form of social life. Discussion among equals replaced mere obedience to a higher authority; solidarity resulted from persuasion rather than force.

A new power made its appearance at this point in time: the power of the spoken word. The Greeks made of it a divinity: Pleitho, the goddess of persuasion. But it was no

longer a matter of words endowed with some religious or
magical sanction. Nor was it the same as the sovereign pro-
nouncements of the kings of Homeric legend. The new concept of law rested on the foundation of free and reasoned
discussion which led to conviction, and through conviction
to decision. All those questions which priests and kings had
formerly settled without possibility of appeal were now submitted to the Assembly, which weighed the various arguments
and settled the issue by bringing it to a vote.

A second characteristic of the Greek *polis* was the publicity
given to all the most important manifestations of civil life.
In place of the decree of the king, reached by a search of his
own conscience or after consultation with his private counselors, all important questions of general interest were
brought into the open and publicly discussed. Little by little
participation in all serious affairs involving the city as a
whole, originally reserved to small aristocratic, religious or
military groups, was extended to members of all classes recognized as having the qualities requisite for citizenship.

A third characteristic was the continuous popular control
of the actions of magistrates. Here we have for the first time
the notion of "accountability," as contrasted to the "good
pleasure" of the king who claimed to rule by divine right, or
to the tyrant who admitted accountability to no one.

A fourth characteristic was that sentiment which the Greeks
described as *isonomia* (there is no exact equivalent in a
Western language)—the notion that every citizen is equal
before the law to every other. Ties of reciprocity replaced the
traditional ties of subordination. Everyone who took part in
the affairs of the state declared himself to be and felt himself
to be an equal among equals.

All these characteristics combined to secularize political
life. The official religion, once intimately involved with
human affairs, became entirely formal; it decorated but did
not determine social life. Its rites, such as the sacrifice or the

oath that magistrates were still obliged to take upon entering office, were no more than a formal framework of public life. The priest became a state official who no longer taught dogma; his task became the management of practical affairs.

With democracy was born a new force—patriotism—conceived not as loyalty to the person of a prince but as a love for the city, a feeling that in defending the city one was defending a part of one's self. The Greeks were convinced that the freer men were, the stronger they were. The Persian Wars affirmed this conviction. How could it have been otherwise when the tiny army of democratic Athens had crushed the enormous Persian war machine?

In becoming a citizen the Greek became a patriot, a far more formidable fighter than the mercenaries whom Asian despots drove doggedly into battle. Mercenaries would never have raised the shout of the Greek sailors at Salamis: "On, sons of Greece, save your native land, rescue your sons, your wives, your temples and the tombs of your ancestors!" [4] The Greek fought with purpose because he fought for home and hearth.

A MONEY ECONOMY

Just as Greek rationalism led to the creation of the demonstrative sciences and to Athenian democracy, so too it led to a radical reorganization of economic life. By the fifth century B.C., Piraeus had become the great storehouse of Greece, playing in the Mediterranean world the role which the City of London was to play in the commerce and economic life of the nineteenth century A.D. This primacy was due, first and foremost, to the scrupulous respect given to private property. Each year, on entering office, the Athenian archon listed the possessions of every citizen and guaranteed him his ownership and rights of disposal.

This primacy was almost equally due to a strong monetary

discipline. If we may believe tradition, it was in Lydia, at the crossroads of the Asiatic and Mediterranean worlds, that King Gyges first issued minted coins. But it was the Greek cities—Argos, Aegina, Corinth and Athens—which were responsible for spreading their use. The Laurium mines provided the Athenians with the silver for their famous drachmas. And never throughout their long history, regardless of the difficulties in which they found themselves, did the Athenians change the legal title or the weight of their money. That is why the Athenian "owls"—the Attic tetradrachmas—became an international money like the English pound in the nineteenth century, right down to the time that Alexander introduced a single money valued according to the Attic unit which provided the basis for the Roman denarius.

At a time when most other Greek cities were still living from the fruits of their lands and the production of their households, the Athenians had developed an exchange economy based on money. The money changers became bankers who accepted deposits, made secured loans, and issued letters of exchange. Athens created a commercial law, inaugurated a system of weights and measures, and established a body of inspectors, called *agoranomoi* and *metronomoi,* to verify the accuracy of weights and the quality of merchandise.

Toward 450 B.C., Athens provided the first example of a state prepared to rely on overseas areas for its food supplies and to pay for these by cultivating a few special crops (vines and olives) and producing manufactured goods best suited to its natural aptitudes and resources (silver, marble, fine ceramic clay). By the fourth century, Athens was importing four times as much food grain as it was producing and was enjoying what we would today call a favorable balance of trade—paying with finished goods, such as vases, jewelry, arms, and fine cloth, for raw materials, food stuffs, metals, gold from Thrace, purple dyes from Phoenicia, hides from Syria, and wheat from Egypt and Scythia. Attic pottery was to be found in the remote steppes of Russia, in the Danube basin and in South Germany. Such distant exchanges were made the easier by the absence of the customs barriers characteristic of later times. For the most part, the only burdens on trade were the light charges made at points of origin and final destination.

Progress in navigation gave the Athenians mastery of the seas, due in part to the increased size of sailing ships and the use of heavily manned oars, and in part to better knowledge of trade routes. This mastery provided still another source of revenue—the tribute paid by allies for protection.

Finally, and in contrast to the other aristocratic cities of Greece, democratic Athens did not despise manual labor and the work of craftsmen. Traders and artisans were citizens; skilled craftsmen from abroad were welcomed. The government contracted for public works with freemen or even with strangers living in the city. The Laurium mines long depended upon the labor of freemen.

In brief, Athens in the period of her greatness had what we today would call a free market economy. And it was this which gave her undisputed leadership in wealth and culture, a leadership that was to survive military defeat and the loss of empire. She could console herself because in losing her empire she did not thereby lose her wealth.

ETHICS AS A SCIENCE

Rationalism did more than govern Greek thinking; it tended also to govern conduct, providing an intellectual foundation for moral views. Socrates taught that virtue is a science and that to know the good is to will the good. The deadly sin was bad judgment. Hence, to quote Epictetus, "One must seek never to be mistaken, never to act impetuously, in a word, never to assent to anything until after due deliberation." [5] This is why the Stoics tied ethics so closely to logic. Since to err was to do evil, it was essential, if one were to avoid evil, to reason correctly, to devote oneself to the study of syllogisms, to the solution of aporias and mastery of the dialectic. Since morality was regarded as a science, it was always praiseworthy to teach it and to bring the wicked back to the paths of righteousness.

The aim of ethics is the realization of the highest good by living in accordance with nature. Since man is by nature reasonable, it follows that life lived in accordance with reason is moral. The virtue held in highest esteem was moderation—control of one's passion, subordination of the faculties to the control of reason. Moderation was an art, the exercise of tact and measure and the avoidance of extremes. Socrates taught that moderation, the golden mean, and the timely word or deed were the greatest of the virtues. To possess inner beauty, to remain master of one's destiny, never to be surprised by events, to be able on the last day of one's existence to give as one's password "calmness," was to have lived the good life guided by wisdom. Other than that, everything was arrogance, folly, and hyperbole. The unforgivable crime was extremism, the Homeric *hubris* which leads the foolish to think they can equal the gods. Zeus's first ironic gift to those he would destroy was the rashness which stems from vanity.

As moderation was the first virtue for the individual, so justice was the first virtue of the citizen. Plato defined justice by appeal to three other virtues—temperance, courage and prudence. Justice was the unifying principle which unites them into a perfect harmony.[6] Harmony was beauty, be it of the soul or of the body. To the Greeks, beauty was a manifestation of the good. Their humanism was summed up in the phrase, "A beautiful soul in a beautiful body."

WRITING AND THE DEMOCRATIZATION OF
GREEK CULTURE

A series of happy accidents accounts for the uniqueness of
Greece. One of the most noteworthy of these was the pho-
neticization of writing in the twelfth and eleventh centuries
B.C.

The Phoenician alphabet, created for the needs of commerce, enriched with vowels by the subtle Greeks, became the
necessary and perfect instrument for communicating ideas.
Twenty-four letters, plus a few accent marks, sufficed to
transcribe all the modulations of the spoken word. From then
on, and without excessive effort, reading came within the
reach of increasing numbers of people; and through the written word, knowledge could be preserved and diffused with
ease.

The writings of the ancient Egyptians consisted of several
hundred pictorial characters which had to be memorized.
Their mastery demanded a long and costly apprenticeship
which few could afford. Scribes were thus a privileged minority in a society of illiterates. Like the Scholastics of the Middle Ages and like the Chinese mandarins, they associated
knowledge with books, to the neglect of experience and the
study of nature. Nothing new was added; the older a manuscript was, the greater the veneration in which it was held.
Tradition and routine prevailed instead of a zest for discovery
and innovation.[7]

How different from the lively discussions which took place
in the market at Athens, among the Sophists gathered at
every public square, and among the philosophers at their
large and public schools. How different from the spirit of
free exchange which led Plato to correspond with his friend
Archytos at Tarente, which led Archimedes of Syracuse to
send his precious manuscript to his colleagues in Alexandria,
which led Apollonius of Pergama to send his treatise on

conic sections to Eudoxus of Rhodes, and which led Alexander to send his collection of animals to his teacher, Aristotle. A constant ferment of ideas spread from city to city; scholars raised problems and intellectuals issued challenges. Small wonder that Greek science progressed rapidly and became truly international; Eratosthenes's measurement of the earth, Hipparchus's map of the heavens, and Ptolemy's map of the earth all required far-flung collaboration which helped spread Greek as the international language of science and made possible the creation at Alexandria of the celebrated Library and Museum where poets, mathematicians, astronomers, doctors, philosophers and philologists lived and worked together.

Knowledge was no longer the private possession of a small conservative class of priests and scribes; it became accessible to wider and wider circles. Had it not been for the revolution in writing, science would necessarily have consisted of a rubble heap of techniques based upon magic formulas and confined to priests and scribes. Never would the world have witnessed what happened in Greece: communities of citizens rejecting the decrees of gods and kings in favor of laws of their own making. Without that revolution in writing, Western civilization would never have been possible.

FREEDOM OF THOUGHT AND THE ABSENCE OF RELIGIOUS DOGMATISM

In Greece, as later in Rome, and contrary to what happened in different Eastern civilizations and in Christian Europe down to the eighteenth century, thought was never subjected to any religious orthodoxy by a religious order with sufficient temporal power to enforce its will. The loose and changing mythologies and archaic rites of pagan religions bore no message of a dogmatic character which could fetter the free development of thought. In Greek cities, religion was purely a ritual and its observance no more than a simple municipal function. True, there were from time to time impulsive outbreaks of religious intolerance. But these trials for religious heresy were in fact no more than chauvinistic outbursts directed against philosophers, who, with the sole exception of Socrates, were aliens. If at times harsh laws were written against freedom of thought, public opinion rarely enforced them.

The sages of Greece based their rejection of the anthropomorphism of the Olympic gods on a higher concept of divinity and the imperatives of ethics as a science.

As a result of his wanderings for sixty-seven years over every part of Greece, Xenophanes of Colophon noted that men everywhere pictured their gods in their own likeness.

Ethiopians have gods with snub noses and black hair; Tracians have gods with gray eyes and red hair . . . If oxen, horses and lions had hands and could paint and sculpt like men, they would depict their gods in their own forms; horses would make gods like horses, and oxen like oxen.[8]

Early man did more than give his gods mortal form; he also endowed them with his feelings, passions and vices. Xenophanes directed his satires against Homer and Hesiod, who "have attributed to the gods all things that are shameful and a reproach among mankind: theft, adultery and mutual deception." [9] On this point, philosophers, dramatists and historians were in agreement. The fables of the poets, Pindar said, were brilliant fantasies "made enchanting by poetry which alone has the power to make believable the implausible." Pindar believed that about the gods "only beautiful things should be told." [10]

But did the gods, even stripped of their all too human attributes, really exist? Democritus regarded them as no more than the products of early man's fear of natural events, which seemed terrifying only because of his inability to explain them. "Our ancestors, on seeing the strange happenings in the heavens, the thunder and lightning, comets and eclipses of the sun and moon, were afraid. They thought that the gods were the causes of these phenomena." [11] The Sophists, noting the diversity of the gods worshiped in different parts of Greece and among the barbarians, did not hesitate to conclude that they were the mere products of conventions and were not to be found in nature. Early lawmakers, according to the Sophists, had developed these gods from their imaginations in order to assure the sanctity of contracts, respect for oaths and maintenance of public order.

A century and a half of reflection had made skeptics of all the best minds in Greece.

THE BALANCE SHEET OF HELLENISM

The Greeks were convinced that their knowledge was vastly superior to that of the barbarians of the East. They were aware of the debt they owed to the East but they knew they had put the loan to good use. No one has made the point better than the Roman emperor Julian. He observed:

Knowledge of celestial phenomena was perfected by the Greeks on the basis of earlier observations made by the Barbarians at Babylon. Geometry, offspring of Egyptian geodesy, produced the enormous improvements that we have witnessed. It was again the Greeks who raised the arithmetic of the Phoenician traders to the status of a science. And finally, it was again the Greeks who, by uniting these three disciplines, applied geometry to astronomy, combined arithmetic with the two and discovered the harmonious relationships which they mutually support.[12]

We have spent so much time on Greek rationalism because it is the foundation on which our Western civilization is built. Without it, the scientific, industrial, and technical revolutions of the seventeenth, eighteenth, and twentieth cen-

turies would not have been possible; the very idea of government by laws publicly discussed and adopted by commonly
accepted procedures would not have arisen. Without it, the
conception of the autonomy of the human person, destined
to develop his faculties and shape his destiny, might never
have prevailed. Without this Greek rationalism we might
never have escaped from myth and magic with all its super-
stitions, taboos and restraints. Perseus slaying Medusa is the
symbol of Greek genius: reason freeing itself from the spell
of fable.

Rationalism was not, of course, the only current operating
in the Greek world. Alongside the spirit of Apollo was the
spirit of Dionysius. With the restraints of wisdom went the
transports of folly. The daring flights of thought of the
Ionians and the Abderites were matched by the sober and
practical morality of Socrates. Alongside the Academy and
the Lyceum, concerned with the world of ideas and of nature,
there was the Eleusium, where men tried to fathom the mysteries of the lower regions. In opposition to Pericles's open
society was Plato's closed society; and opposing the research
institutes of the Peripatetics was the mysticism of Plotinus
and the theurgy of Porphyry. He who would understand
Greece in all its imperishable aspects is like Faust before the
sorcerer's mirror, seeing the reflection of his own desires. For
some, the true Greece is that of the great tragedies, the
Dionysian frenzy, the Heraclitian flux, and the *amor fati,* or
fascination with fate; for others, it is the Greece of the Muses,
of the laurels of Apollo and of eternal serenity. For still
others, the great forerunners are the Ionian physiocrats, Em-
pedocles and the school of the Atomists, who explained the
world as the plaything of fate and chance; while for another
group the truly great are Pythagoras, Plato and Plotinus, who
portray the world as divinely ordained and eternal. Some
insist that the flat-nosed and freckled Socrates with his suppressed passions was the great corrupter of Greek traditions;

others see him as the finest embodiment of classical Greece because he brought out the existence of an inner beauty more lovely than any external beauty visible to the senses. One group makes its pilgrimage to the theater of Dionysius at the foot of the Acropolis; another climbs the Pantheon to the temple of Athena; and still another pushes on to Sparta, while regretting some distant Thule.

For our purposes it is enough to recall those aspects of the Greek mind without which Western civilization could never have come into existence. Other civilizations made important contributions in their way. But it remained for the Greeks to give meaning to the word *Logos,* a characteristic of human behavior they cherished most highly: reason and reasoning, word and speech, ratio and proportion.

No one has better summed up the Greek contribution to Western civilization than Ernest Renan:

Our science, our arts, our literature, our philosophy, our moral code, our political code, our strategy, our diplomacy, our maritime and international law are of Greek origin. The framework of human culture created by Greece is susceptible of indefinite enlargement, but it is complete in itself in its several parts. Progress will consist in constantly developing what Greece has conceived, in executing the design which she has, so to speak, traced out for us.[13]

III

ROMAN ORDER

ROMAN LAW

If the Greek contribution to Western civilization was the establishment of the principle of liberty, Rome's was the establishment of the principle of order. Without order, liberty degenerates into license, and democracy into anarchy. To define for each man and for each situation what is legal and to fix for each private and public act its proper procedure is an indispensable protection against arbitrary power. Law enables men to know what their rights and duties are, what manner of behavior they are expected to follow in the countless situations which arise in family and social life, and what the public powers will and will not do.[1]

If law is to protect the citizen against all acts of arbitrary power, it is essential that it be codified in a precise and well-organized form. True, certain lawmakers, like Hammurabi and Solon and the authors of Leviticus, had elaborated small bodies of law. But no people have realized the immense coordination and unification of law to which Roman lawyers devoted themselves from very early times down to Justinian. The *Codes*, the *Digest* and the *Institutes* are in truth the legal heritage of the West.

No less remarkable than the codification of Roman law was its increasingly humane and universal character. In the very early days there were two legal jurisdictions, one of which involved matters touching citizens, the other of which decided issues between citizens and foreigners. The first constituted civil law, the second the law of nations. The law for citizens, derived as it was from the Law of the Twelve Tables, was so encumbered with traditions and superstitious rules that it forced the praetors to correct the injustices by appeals to equity. The disrespect in which the old law was held is suggested by the proverb, *summum jus, summa injuria*—the more perfectly the law is enforced, the greater the injustice. The second body of law, free of national prejudice and ancestral custom, focused on merchants and other aliens temporarily domiciled in Rome. It was simpler, more humane and more reasonable. As Rome extended the boundaries of the City to the limits of the Empire, the law of nations supplanted the civil law and became, in effect, Roman law.

The principle of this Roman law tended increasingly to be identified with the natural law which the Stoic philosophers regarded as a moral code implanted in all beings endowed with reason, hence valid in all circumstances. The jurist Ulpien deduced from it the revolutionary conclusion that class distinctions and privileges were artificial and accidental, since according to natural law all men are equal. Roman law aspired to be "reason in writing." Cicero developed this conception in a passage which was to inspire the whole Western legal tradition:

True law is right reason in agreement with nature; it is of universal application, immutable and eternal. . . . We are not allowed to alter this law, nor is it allowable to attempt to repeal any part of it, and it is impossible to abolish it entirely. We cannot be freed from its obligations by Senate or by people, and we need not look outside ourselves for an interpreter of it. There is not a different law for Rome and for Athens, or one for now and one for the future, but one eternal and unchangeable law valid for all nations and all times. . . . Whoever is disobedient is fleeing from himself and denying his human nature.[2]

The idea, propounded by later scholars like Grotius, that there are rights which belong originally and essentially to the very nature of man, drew its inspiration from Cicero and the great Roman jurists, and in due time was to inspire many others: John Locke, the philosophers of the eighteenth century, and the fathers of the American and the French revolution. It led to the *Declaration of the Rights of Man and of the Citizen,* which in turn inspired all the constitutions of the nineteenth and twentieth centuries.

ROMAN UNIVERSALISM

What Greece conceived and fitted to the requirements of small city-states, Rome, faithful to its calling as pacifier and administrator of peoples through law, extended to the limits of its empire. The celebrated verses of Vergil sum up Rome's historic mission:

> *Remember Roman, you are to rule the peoples,*
> *Give the laws and make the peace,*
> *Save the vanquished and humble the proud.*[3]

The Romans believed themselves predestined for empire, but what is admirable in their case is not that they established an empire but that they knew so well how to preserve it. The despots of Asia knew how to conquer peoples, but the Oriental empires were precarious because they invited rebellion, resting as they did on repression and servitude. The city of Romulus succeeded in constructing a stable empire because she knew how to treat the conquered as associates, allies and friends. She thus progressively extended her laws, first to the peoples of Latium, then to all of Italy, and finally to the provinces. Claudius explained, when demanding that the bearded Gauls be granted citizenship: "Why did the Lacedaemons and the Athenians, once so powerful in arms, perish if it was not because they rejected the conquered as foreigners? Whereas our founder, Romulus, with much better wisdom, fought and naturalized a people in the course of the same day." [4]

By the beginning of the second century B.C. the Empire had become a federation of cities, all governed by the same laws and by the same administration, grouped around the most powerful of them, Rome, the tutor and lawmaker of the world. Instead of having one law for strangers and another for Latins, there was only one law—Roman law. Instead of exploiting the provinces by right of conquest, Rome offered protection of their rights by virtue of the law of nations.

It was thanks to this policy of assimilation that Rome was able to bring civilization to the rude peoples she conquered. Rather than spreading around herself in ever-widening circles the solitude of deserted lands and the silence of the tomb, she renewed herself and her ruling classes through the influx of people from the provinces.

No sooner does one voice die down in this symphony of peoples than another arises at the command of the magic baton of the orchestra leader at Rome. The earliest rough melodies came from the writers of Latium, followed by the more disciplined writers of the cities of central Italy—Lucretius, Cicero, Caesar, and Varro. Then literary supremacy moves to the beautiful cisalpine lands with Vergil, Vetruvius, and Catullus. Here enter the harmonic voices of Gaul and the Spain of Seneca. As these are muted, the melody passes to Africa, amplified by a revival of Greek letters under the Antonines in Helles and Syria.

Rome planted her courts, her baths, her libraries, and her theaters throughout the Mediterranean basin and transformed it into a peaceful forum where the ideas, customs and products of three continents were exchanged.

The City (*urbs*) became the Universe (*orbis*) because it knew how to expand its walls to encompass an empire. And in the process the world lost some of its ancient harshness. It turned from its manlike goddesses, who, from the heights of the Acropolis, shook their lances, to the more peaceful and reasonable Muses. The verses of Vergil and Tibullus sang the melancholy of human tenderness; concern for the poor and sympathy for the afflicted were no longer treated as a sign of weakness. Medical health services were organized for the poor; money grants were made to needy families to help them bring up their children; pure water was made available to homes for a small fee. The great jurists declared slavery to be contrary to nature; imperial laws recognized the slave as a person and created a special office charged with protecting his interests.

In destroying the particularism of cities, with their quarrelsome local patriotisms and their exclusive municipal religions, Rome created the idea of a universal state and a world citizenship. "To be a Roman," declared Aelius Aristides, "no longer means to be from a certain city; it means to be of one great family." [5]

An obscure poet from conquered Gaul sang this tribute to Rome's power and humanism: "You have given a fatherland to diverse peoples . . . and, allowing the vanquished to share your rights, you have created a single city." [6]

The great historian Rudolph von Ihering has given us an apposite summary of the Roman mission:

Rome represents the triumph of the idea of universality over the principle of nationality. . . . A nation which isolates itself not only commits a crime against itself, since it deprives itself of the means for perfecting its own development, but it also is guilty of an injustice against other peoples. Isolation is the capital crime of peoples, for the supreme law of history is community.[7]

Rome created ecumenism—the unity toward which people surfeited with war will never cease to aspire. The universality of Rome inspired the ideal of "one world," originally a

Roman world, but in time and as a result of the conquests of Charlemagne, a Christian world.[8] The airplane and communication satellites have completed the physical unification of the world begun by the Romans with their network of roads. As the earth grows smaller it cries out for international organization to regulate the life of humanity by law.

THE "PAX ROMANA"

Needless to say, the *Pax Romana,* as long as it was effective, permitted an enormous expansion in economic life which was felt well beyond the Mediterranean basin. Roman gold coins have been found along the coast of Mysore, in Ceylon and in Indochina. Commerce extended from the equator in the Sudan to the remote borders of Tibet and Siberia. It was promoted by the great public works which the imperial government supported; the excellent network of roads, the sea lanes cleared of pirates, the aqueducts and safe harbors, the quarries and mines, and the frontier fortifications which protected the Empire against barbarian invasion. Many of the countries bordering on the Mediterranean have not regained in eighteen centuries the level of economic activity they enjoyed during this period. Indeed, according to Winston Churchill,

Britain, reconciled to the Roman system, enjoyed in many respects, the happiest, most comfortable, and most enlightened times its inhabitants have ever had. . . . There was a sense of pride in sharing so noble and widespread a system. To be a citizen of Rome was to be a citizen of the world, raised upon a pedestal of unquestioned superiority above barbarians and slaves. Movement across the great Empire was as rapid as when Queen Victoria came to the throne, and no obstruction of frontiers, laws, currency, or nationalism hindered it.[9]

To understand the magnitude of this economic expansion, one has only to compare Strabo's world of the first century

A.D. with that of Ptolemy 150 years later. Strabo's map does not go beyond India and Ceylon; Ptolemy's shows Indochina and the southern coastline of China.

The Roman Empire provided an exceptionally favorable environment for bringing together a wide range of human experience. Merchants, craftsmen, public officials, and slaves were constantly traveling the great highways of the Empire. Soldiers, recruited from every province, were stationed in regions which they could never otherwise have hoped to see. Missionaries and ambassadors from distant lands followed the same routes as the merchants and the soldiers, and all roads led to Rome.

Under the rule of the Antonines, who put the ablest men in the highest posts, it seemed as though the age of gold sung by the poets was about to return.

IV

THE HANDICAP
OF ANCIENT CIVILIZATIONS:
SLAVERY

WHY THE SCIENTIFIC KNOWLEDGE OF THE GREEKS
DID NOT LEAD TO AN INDUSTRIAL REVOLUTION

It would have been logical for Greek genius, benefiting from the protective shield provided by the Roman Empire, to have realized the scientific and industrial revolution accomplished in the seventeenth and succeeding centuries.[1] Why didn't it occur?

One theory has it that the Greeks, absorbed by the play of pure thought, were neither observers nor experimenters. The astronomy of Hipparchus, the geography of Eratosthenes and Ptolemy, the works of the Greek historians, the medicine of Hippocrates and Galen, the zoology of Aristotle, and the botany of Theophastus all presumed, however, the gathering of a considerable number of observations. Ingenious tools were also invented: the worm screw, the cog wheel, gears, pumps, cranes, presses, and instruments for measuring the stars. There were impressive works of engineering such as the mile-long Samos tunnel, which was started simultaneously from opposite sides of the mountain. Why did this technical knowledge not then lead to a scientific revolution?

SLAVERY DISCREDITED THE MECHANICAL ARTS

The most fundamental reason is to be found in an institution present in all ancient societies, an institution which prevented the development of machinery and the applied sciences—human slavery. The lack of machinery, by an inevitable vicious circle, so increased the need for slavery as to make it appear to be established by nature. Manual work, because it was performed mostly by slaves, discredited craftsmanship and the mechanical arts. The attention of citizens and scholars was turned away from anything involving the work of the hands; science took a speculative turn without regard for practical applications which might have reduced human suffering and improved the human condition.

Slavery, paradoxical as it may seem, was not a step backward in man's evolution. In the wars of primitive tribes, all male prisoners were put to the sword. Slavery developed when it was realized that a defeated enemy was more valuable alive than dead. It was an outcome of man's growing rationality, a product of self-interest rather than pity. Soon slaves were purposefully acquired by means of piracy. Another source of slaves was through breeding; the child of a woman slave belonged to her master. Finally, an insolvent debtor could in most Greek cities be sold as a slave. In Athens, the reforms of Solon (594 B.C.) forbade seizure of the person for debts.

Although preferable to death, slavery had little else to offer the vanquished. The slave was not considered a human being; he had no legal existence. He could be sold, bequeathed, rented out, or given away. In the hands of his master he was a thing, a "living tool," as Aristotle said.[2] His fate depended on the discretion of the owner. The Greeks, and particularly the Athenians, actually treated their slaves less harshly than their laws might imply. Dressed in the same way as their masters, they are shown in Greek comedies speaking blunt truths without fear. They were admitted to numerous religious ceremonies on a footing of equality. They enjoyed certain guarantees: the law forbade a master to kill his slave, required an owner to sell a slave who had taken refuge in a temple, and fixed the maximum physical punishment at fifty lashes.

In rural Greece there were few slaves. The small landowner preferred to cultivate his land himself, and slave labor was too costly. Nor in the beginning were there many slaves in the cities. In early Athens the work of the artisan was held in honor. There was even a law requiring citizens to learn a trade.

But as production for wider markets developed, slavery increased and working conditions deteriorated, particularly in the mines. In the fourth century B.C., Demetrius of Phalerum spoke of 25,000 citizens and 400,000 slaves in Athens—although these figures are certainly exaggerated. Working in groups in urban shops, slaves lacked the human warmth of family life. And attitudes changed. Manual labor, regarded as destructive of the beauty of the body, came also to be regarded as destructive of the mind and soul.[3]

In effect, the Greek citizen became a sort of *rentier,* freed from the tasks of providing for himself his food, clothing, and housing. Spartan law even forbade the citizen from doing productive work of any kind. At Thespiae, it was regarded as a disgrace to learn a trade or to cultivate the land. At Thebes, shopkeepers and petty traders could hold public office only ten years after retiring from business. In most of the aristocratic cities, citizenship was incompatible with the exercise of a manual profession.

Prejudice against the mechanical arts became so strong that Archimedes, the inventor of the lever, wedge, pulley, worm screw, and winch, would not—if we may believe Plutarch—leave behind any written treatise on these matters: "regarding the work of an engineer and every art that ministers to the needs of life as ignoble and vulgar, he devoted his earnest efforts only to those studies the charm and subtlety of which are not affected by the claims of necessity." [4]

There was indeed a celebrated school of engineering at Alexandria. But the work emerging from this school aimed at amusing the great and wealthy. It did not occur to the engineers to use the power of water, compressed air, or steam, which they had learned to control, to make machines capable of lightening men's heavy tasks.

The most significant example of their ingenuity was the eolipile, a device they used to make balls spin, marionettes dance, and toy trumpets blow. It involved the same principle as the steam engine James Watt rediscovered centuries later. Yet its inventor, Heron, evidently never gave a passing thought to the way in which it could have been made into a turbine to relieve the task of the workers, nor did he even think of lightening one of the most exhausting tasks of antiquity—the grinding of grain—a task which fell for the most part on women.

ARISTOTLE'S JUSTIFICATION OF SLAVERY

In order that a privileged few might taste the joys of pure knowledge, the need for slavery was taken for granted. Both Plato and Aristotle argued for it on the grounds of nature and necessity. Slavery is a natural right, observed Aristotle in his *Politics:* "He who can foresee by the exercise of his mind is by nature intended to be lord and master, and he who can with his body give effect to such foresight is a subject and by nature a slave." [5] Aristotle did of course recognize two distinct situations: slavery by nature and slavery by accident, such as in the vicissitudes of war. But he passed very lightly over the problem of slavery by accident and hastened on to his second, and to him irrefutable, argument from necessity:

. . . no man can live well, or indeed live at all, unless he is provided with necessaries. And as in the arts which have a definite sphere, the workers must have their own proper tools for the accomplishment of their work, so it is in the management of a household. Now tools are of various sorts; some are living, others are lifeless . . . in the arrangement of the family, a slave is a living tool.[6]

These "living tools" were deemed necessary for both the household and the state. The only escape from this rule of necessity was mentioned ironically as utopian, a madman's dream:

Of course, if every instrument could accomplish its own work, obeying or anticipating the will of others . . . if the shuttle would weave and the plectrum touch the lyre without a hand to guide them, foremen would not want servants, nor masters slaves.[7]

History would in due time show that mankind would have to wait for the power loom, the steam engine, the internal combustion engine, the turbine, and cybernetic machines until human bondage had largely disappeared. The ancient world, however, regarded slavery as a permanent part of the natural order. "Nowhere," observed Gaston Bossier, "in the writings of antiquity do we find expressed as a distant hope or a passing wish, or even as a plausible hypothesis, the idea that slavery can someday be suppressed." [8]

Again, Aristotle's attitude is illuminating; he thought technology and the applied sciences had completed their tasks and there was nothing left to invent which could add to the comfort of life. Accordingly, Aristotle invited all freemen, and especially the young, to leave to slaves and insignificant artisans the responsibility for providing for mundane things, and to devote themselves to disinterested activities, speculative science, and, above all, philosophy. In his view none of these concerned itself with the necessities or material amenities of life.

THE DECLINE OF THE SCIENTIFIC SPIRIT

By discrediting manual labor, slavery discredited the applied sciences and thus blocked scientific progress on almost all fronts.

The physical sciences can progress only by solving problems of practical application—the construction, for example, of the observing and measuring instruments which make experimentation possible. But for the art of pouring and cutting glass, there would have been no telescope, no microscope, no test tube, no thermometer, no barometer, and therefore no physics of gases, no theory of heat, no chemistry, no astronomy, no microphysics or microbiology.

The scientific spirit which had flowered during the Hellenic period declined during the Roman epoch. Education became purely literary. After the young Roman had mastered grammar, which taught him to write and speak correctly and acquainted him with the classical authors, he went to a school of oratory which taught him the art and practice of eloquence. In possession of this art of oratory, the Roman felt himself master of the world even as he was master of the verb. Public speaking, Quintilian declared, opened up to him "power, honors, friendships and glory in this world and in the world to come." [9] There was nothing which prompted the young Roman to cultivate the sciences; everything pushed him toward the pursuit of honors in public life.

And all this happened when the facilities available to the citizens of the Empire were more abundant than ever before. Libraries had multiplied; government offices had established archives; the known world had been enormously expanded. Never before had there been so many people of both education and leisure and so many contacts with the world outside the Empire. Nonetheless, the golden age of the creative spirit was over. Such curiosity as remained found expression in encyclopedic but unoriginal compilations. Seneca, Pliny the

Elder, Strabo and Galen devoted their great talents to a study of the past; their minds were closed to the future. It was a time of summing up and accounting for past accomplishments.

During the third and fourth centuries, the scientific retreat became a rout as men's interests turned increasingly to religious issues. The last great Greek school of philosophy, the Neoplatonic, gave way to schools concerned with metaphysical vaporizings which led the human spirit back to the age of myth and magic. Pseudosciences, astrology and divination, flourished. Nature was transformed into a vast symbolism, the meaning of which was to be discovered through allegory. It was the collapse of the scientific spirit.

In Greco-Roman times, the factor necessary for the realization of the scientific and technical revolution was lacking, just as it was lacking in the Chinese and Hindu civilizations. The missing element was the idea of progress.[10] In its stead antiquity offered the idea of a humanity which emerges step by step from primitive savagery, reaches a summit, and then declines and disappears. This Roman idea differed sharply from the notion of endless progression held by Condorcet and the philosophers of the Enlightenment. Insofar as Romans like the poet Lucretius grasped this idea it was in the moral sphere; Lucretius saw the possibility that pagan fear of the gods and of sanctions from beyond the tomb might eventually be banished from the human soul, but he expected no improvement in the human condition from industrial and technical progress. Like Socrates, the Epicureans, and the Stoics, he based happiness on the correct appreciation of good and evil, on the struggle against human passions, on the elimination of useless needs, and on resources to be found within the self. The wise man knew it was better to restrict his wants than to try to change the world. *Sustine, abstine* (endure, do without) remained the maxim of wisdom in antiquity.[11]

THE REVENGE OF SPARTACUS

By curbing science and technology, slavery became the nemesis of the societies which accepted it as natural and necessary. It brought ruin to the Greek cities, to the Hellenic empire, and finally to Rome, by creating an expansive urban proletariat and by impoverishing the agrarian masses. The processes which led to the collapse were much the same everywhere. Wars increased the number of slaves, and their competition as laborers drove the small-scale producers and petty traders of the cities into the ranks of the proletariat. The same competition forced small peasant landholders to sell their holdings to rich neighbors, who pieced together great estates cultivated by slaves.

The plight of the landless peasant in Italy was vividly pictured by Tiberius Gracchus (133 B.C.) in his speech on behalf of agrarian reform:

In Italy wild animals have their dens, but the men who fight and die for Italy have only the light and the air they breathe; they wander about homeless with their wives and children. The generals who exhort them to fight for their tombs and temples are lying; for there is not one among these many Romans who still has an hereditary altar or an ancestral tomb. But they fight and die to support others in wealth and luxury, and though they are called the masters of the world, they do not even own a lump of earth.[12]

Small wonder many of these landless peasants flocked to Rome, swelling the ranks of impoverished plebs from Greece, Syria, Egypt, Africa, and Spain—men who had been torn from their countries, sold as slaves, and later freed by their masters and made Roman citizens. Unable to support themselves, they turned to the state for food, shelter, and amusement—*panem et circenses.* "Most heads of families," a contemporary reported, "slipped within our walls leaving behind their scythes and plows. They prefer to clap their hands at the circus rather than to work in their fields and vineyards." [13]

The pleb brought in his wake a threefold corruption: electoral, senatorial, and military. Candidates for public office bought plebeian votes with spectacles, public dinners, and distributions of free food. Increasingly, senators came to think of the state as their private property, to be drawn upon freely to cover their gifts to the electorate and to maintain their large establishments. Some senators sent to the provinces as governors extracted ransom from them; others demanded bribes from foreign kings for protection. Finally, the army became corrupted. In the early days, the army was made up of peasants who were both citizens and soldiers; like Cincinnatus, they fought for their country and then returned to their fields. But as the numbers of these citizen-soldiers declined, generals admitted to their legions destitute citizens who enrolled in the hope of making a fortune through pillage. They were no longer soldiers from a sense of duty; soldiering had become a career.

These professionals recognized neither the senate nor the law; they obeyed only their generals. Ordinary citizens like Pompey and Crassus, enriched with spoils from the provinces, raised armies at their own expense. There were four such armies in existence in 78 B.C.

With the senate stripped of all moral authority, there remained only one real force in the society, the army, and it was corrupt. The stage was set for the civil wars which would bury the Republic. Pliny the Elder was right when he said that the large estates had destroyed Italy. What he did not recognize was that these estates were the result of the wars of conquest and the institution of slavery.

Caesar and Augustus ended the civil wars—and the Republic. They gave the Empire an administration which was relatively honest and efficient. More important, they restored peace which lasted for the better part of two and a half centuries. An era of prosperity opened, sung by Vergil and Horace as a return to the golden age. Cities sprang up in the new provinces and population increased in Gaul, Germany, Britain, Spain and Africa. An admirable network of roads promoted the movement of men and goods. Piracy was suppressed and ports multiplied along the seacoasts. Yet the Empire, despite a class of wealthy and cultivated men of leisure, made practically no contributions to the fundamental sciences. The aristocratic prejudice which regarded the mechanical arts as fit only for slaves and freedmen stifled technological progress and discouraged investment in industry. It was even illegal for senators to engage in business.

Once the limits of the Empire were staked out around 150 A.D., the economy was forced to turn inward. To make progress, it would have to render the lower classes productive so that they could at once create wealth and consume it. This never happened. The number of parasites which the Empire had to support grew larger and larger while the productive middle class grew smaller and smaller. By 250 A.D. the Roman economy was bankrupt. When war started again with the Parthians in the East and the Germans who had crossed the Rhine and the Danube, it became necessary to maintain a permanent standing army recruited from barbarian mercenaries. To maintain this army it was necessary to increase taxes and to resort to repeated devaluations, which destroyed the currency as a medium of exchange and forced a return to barter and payments in kind.

The leading classes in the cities were the first to be hurt. Men who had formerly vied with one another for public office now sought only to escape the burden. To become a member of the curia led to almost certain bankruptcy because the state held that body responsible for collecting taxes and making up deficits. Commerce and industry declined; roads fell into disrepair; population in both towns and cities declined. To meet the crisis, the later Empire resorted to totalitarian planning, an ancient remedy known to the Egyptians in the Hellenic age and one which has invariably proved worse than the disease.

The peasant was bound to the land and became a serf. The artisan was forced into a compulsory association or corporation, frequently branded with a hot iron and required to marry within his corporation, which became, in effect, a hereditary caste. The holders of certain public offices were riveted to them and when nominations were made a man could not refuse to serve. The Empire was transformed into one wasteful workshop where everyone worked for the state under bureaucratic supervision. The edict of Diocletian fixed wages and prices throughout this vast estate.

Everyone was caught up in the machinery of an administration which was inquisitorial, inefficient, and unproductive. Life became so unsupportable that people like Orose de Salvien in the fifth century saw no other escape than through appeal to the barbarians. When the great invasion started and dismemberment of the Empire began, Greco-Roman civilization had already been dead for 150 years.

Rome had preferred the slothful and unjust solution offered by slavery instead of trying to develop a technology which could make life easier for the masses. Rome had preferred to entrust the safety of the Empire to barbarians—men of the same race as their slaves—instead of imposing military service on all her citizens. Is it any wonder 40,000 slaves enlisted under the banner of Alaric when he marched on Rome? For having denied its slaves all hope, Rome, the city which had thought itself eternal, saw Spartacus join forces with the barbarians to bring down its columns.

THE SOCIAL REVOLUTION
OF CHRISTIANITY

Greek genius created *homo sapiens* who invented demonstrative science and organized the city rationally. It was not capable of creating *homo faber,* the craftsman, who, by the mechanical arts, mastered the forces of nature and forced them into the service of men. Before he could appear there had to be a moral and social revolution which would abolish slavery and rehabilitate manual labor and the mechanical arts. This was accomplished by Christianity.

THE MORAL REHABILITATION OF THE SLAVE

The Christian message was not intended to reform society. Its purpose was to announce the imminence of the Kingdom of God and the necessity of preparing for it by penitence. While waiting for the great judgment, each person was to remain in the condition where God had placed him. Saint Paul recommended to slaves that they be obedient to their masters, and to masters that they be good to their slaves.

Everyone should remain in the state in which he was called. Were you a slave when called? Never mind. But if you can gain your freedom, avail yourself of the opportunity. For he who was called in the Lord as a slave is a freedman of the Lord. Likewise he who was free when called is a slave of Christ.[1]

[44]

The Letter to the Ephesians recommends: "Masters, do the same to them, and forbear threatening, knowing that he who is both their Master and yours is in heaven, and that there is no partiality with him." [2] It never occurred to the Fathers of the Church, any more than it did to the pagan philosophers and jurisconsults, to envisage the disappearance of slavery. Saint John Chrysostom was content to urge moderation: "Why so many slaves? Just as for your clothing and for the table, you should limit yourself to the number of slaves necessary." [3] Seneca treated his slaves as "humble friends."

Juridically, the slave in antiquity was a thing, a bit of merchandise to be used and abused at will. Aristotle had defined a slave as a "living tool." Slaves were classified for tax purposes in the same category as horses or mules. The slave had no will of his own; he was a body without the power to say no; he had no rights; he had neither family nor legal marriage nor recognized paternity. For him nothing commanded by his master could be shameful. His religion was not recognized; the gods did not concern themselves with slaves. The master could punish him, chain him, imprison, mutilate and torture him, and put him to death.

It was not until the time of the Antonines that a protective office was created to give slaves an appeal to justice against the worst excesses. The great jurisconsults, the Cynics and the Stoics, said all men were born free; they justified slavery, however, by citing the diversified origins of the human family. Some were descended from the gods and heroes and had the right to command. Others were freemen enjoying civil and political rights, divided during the late Empire into men of noble birth (*honestiores*) and men of humble birth (*humiliores*). Still others—by nature, conquest, or birth— were slaves.

Legislation regarding slaves was humanized under the pagan Roman emperors, but under the early Christian emperors there was a retrogression. Constantine revived an old law according to which a free woman cohabiting with a slave would fall under the servitude of that slave's master, and any woman who lived in concubinage with her own slaves was to be burned at the stake. The social order appeared to rest upon slavery.

Nevertheless, Christianity, by declaring that all men descended from the same couple, that they were all children of God, all equally redeemed by the passion of Christ, and all equally worthy as brothers, established the equal dignity of men without exception of condition, race or nationality.

"There is neither Jew nor Greek, there is neither slave nor free, there is neither male nor female; for you are all one in Christ Jesus," proclaimed Saint Paul.[4] The Christian slave is, before God, the equal of the rich man, of the free man, and of his own master. He is admitted on a footing of complete equality into the Church, the love feasts, to the sacraments, into the ranks of the religious hierarchy, and finally to burial in the catacombs. If baptized, he could even be superior to his own master, were the master still an initiate (*catechumen*) or under a public penance. A slave can become a priest, a bishop, even a pope like Calixtus, the escaped slave. His marriage is valid; his paternity is recognized; his chastity is defended; the Christian family is founded.

The Church recommended the freeing of slaves as the highest form of almsgiving and the most acceptable form of penitence; it condemned the enslavement of prisoners; it pledged its resources to the redemption of captives; and it adopted abandoned children. It taught a new respect for the human person, and the Christian emperors, although it is true that they frequently faltered, finally suppressed the gladiatorial combats and the abominable circuses where the blood of the martyrs had flowed so freely. Christianity revolutionized the social positions of slaves and the *humiliores* by providing religious sanctions for their individual dignity; each man, made in the image of God, possessed a free soul.

THE REHABILITATION OF MANUAL LABOR AND THE MECHANICAL ARTS

The proclamation of the equal dignity of all men led inevitably to the rehabilitation of manual labor and the mechanical arts. Was not Jesus a carpenter, the first disciples humble fishermen, and Saint Paul a tent maker? Small wonder that it was among the slaves and the masses of poor laborers that Christianity gained its first great successes.[5] The term *operarius* (laborer) appears frequently in the epitaphs of the Christians. One of the recurring recommendations of the Church was that the artisan should perform his work with zeal and diligence.

The ancients believed a freeman ought to be a man of independent means and leisure, so that he could devote his energies to affairs of state. This was a very different sort of leisure from that of the masses of freemen crowded into the great cities of Imperial Rome. Competition from slave labor had driven from the countryside an army of impoverished peasants, laborers, and artisans. Uprooted and without work, they lived in idleness on public doles, on gratuitous distributions, and on the proceeds of political corruption, passing their days at the theater, the circus, or the amphitheater, demanding *panem et circenses*. The early Christians opposed this corrupting idleness, declaring, in the words of Paul, that "If any one will not work, let him not eat." [6]

Bishops and priests gave the example. Primitive discipline laid upon them the duty of working with their hands. The monks of the West, by introducing manual labor into their monastic rules, made work a part of the *opus Dei*—work of God. One sees them clearing forests, draining swamps, transforming marshy woods into cultivated farms and abbeys, which in turn became the sites of towns, villages, and finally of great cities.

Throughout the Middle Ages, the work of laborers and

artisans was honored on an equal footing with that of other public functionaries. Their organizations—their guilds and corporations—had their own banners which they were entitled to unfurl during the solemn masses devoted to their patron saints. With their own lands and funds, they built the churches, guild halls, and other structures that related in brick and stone and marble the great events of their cities. In time they became powerful enough to extract from kings, feudal lords, and church dignitaries political privileges for themselves. In some places, particularly in Flanders, Germany, and Italy, they actually governed cities. Venice in the thirteenth century was ruled by an aristocracy of merchants. Here was something men of antiquity could not have conceived—cities governed by artisans and merchants.

INVENTIONS IN THE MIDDLE AGES

This glorification of skilled work was one of the factors responsible for the long series of very useful inventions perfected during the Middle Ages.

At the very beginning came the water mill and the windmill. These two forms of energy—of water and of air—dominated technical evolution into the eighteenth century. During the tenth and eleventh centuries rapidly flowing streams were widely exploited for water power, prompting a veritable industrial revolution. The development of the camshaft, which converted circular motion into linear motion —a process known to the ancients but not utilized by them— enabled men to accomplish a great variety of tasks. Hydraulic hammers not only replaced the ancient use of hands and feet but also greatly increased the quality of forged objects. The textile industry particularly benefited from the new machines. A mechanical mill for winding silk appeared in the north of Italy at the end of the twelfth century. Windmills, widely used by the Arabs, developed rapidly after the eleventh century. They were used not only to grind wheat, but also, and especially in the Low Countries, to drain swamps and extract peat.

When Europe started covering itself with a white robe of cathedrals and when the great nobles began to build their fortified castles, new demands were placed upon builders. Very sophisticated lifting tools were developed, using levers, counterweights, and catches. The lifting jack dates from this period. In the notebooks of Villard de Honnecourt we find a design for the jackscrew.

Thanks to machines for lifting weights and draining water, great advances were made in the art of mining. Agriculture also was greatly improved through the development of plows with wheels, moldboards, and plowshares, all of which permitted deeper and more efficient tilling of the soil. The practice of rotating crops every three years greatly increased the production of protein-rich vegetables. These improvements freed more and more of the people from the necessity of working the soil and increased the number who could live in towns and cities. On top of all this, the transportation of people and produce was revolutionized by two innovations: the horse collar, which increased the pulling power of animals, and the fixed rudder, which revolutionized navigation.

Thus in agriculture, mining, animal husbandry, metallurgy, chemistry, armament, and building, considerable progress was made. Taking shape was a technical civilization destined to transform economic and social life and man's view of the world. This development was greatly aided by the gradual disappearance of slavery and by the establishment of relative security from invasion as great feudal monarchies emerged from the eleventh century on.

The religious orders played an important role in these changes. The rule of Saint Benedict, for example, had this to say about work: "If the brothers, whether it be from necessity or from poverty, are obliged to go out to harvest crops themselves, let them not be distressed, for it is when they live by the work of their hands that they will in truth be monks, following the example of our fathers (of the desert) and of the Apostles." [7] The elaborate liturgy to which the Benedictine monks devoted so much of their time required that they shift to the backs of their tenants most of the heavy work which should have been a source of joy to them. Out of this came the Cistercian reforms in the early twelfth century, and the decision by Saint Bernard to emphasize manual labor and the provision by monasteries for all their own needs.

The rule of Saint Bernard stressed the desirability of setting up Cistercian abbeys in areas well supplied with water; the Cistercians were expert in its use for irrigation and the generation of power. The abbey at Foigny possessed fourteen wheat mills, three smelters, three forges, a brewhouse, three presses, and a glass works, all dependent on the power of running water. The first known iron mills were all built by the Cistercians. This order was also responsible for the wide expansion of the three-year crop rotation.

In spite of the interminable wars and disasters like the Black Death, the fourteenth and fifteenth centuries witnessed technical developments destined to revolutionize industrial and commercial life. During these two centuries the consumption of metal for agriculture, industry, and new sorts of artillery (following the introduction by the Arabs of gunpowder from China) increased enormously. Pig iron furnaces and hydraulic forges appeared which doubled iron production and devoured the forests upon which the new metalworking industries depended for fuel. Metallurgy could not really develop, however, until charcoal was replaced by coal, which began in England in 1570.

With the introduction of the fixed rudder, the astrolabe borrowed from the Arabs, the compass imported from China, and the improvements in ship construction which produced the caravel (a fast-sailing ship capable of breasting ocean waves at six leagues an hour), the great adventures of Spanish and Portuguese sailors began. In search of rare spices, they made discoveries which changed man's image of the earth, created empires, and opened commerce between Europe and the New World, the previously unknown Africa, and distant Asia.

A new class appeared, composed of rich merchants and bankers who felt themselves honored to be allowed to embellish their cities. The results can be seen at Augsburg, Bruges, Ghent, Genoa, Florence and Venice. With the development of urban life and luxury, a new humanism began to challenge the Christian humanism which had hitherto dominated the mind of Europe. Instead of exalting poverty as an evangelical virtue and focusing all their attention on personal salvation, men began to live by a new set of values which found in wealth, culture, and beauty the fulfillment of earthly life. They exalted what they called *virtu*—the force of character displayed by the merchant struggling with the hazards of the sea, by noblemen contending with intrigues at court, and by all those men who dared force fortune to their own advantage.

Two other inventions of this period were of the greatest importance: the making of paper, and the science of printing as devised by Gutenberg around the middle of the fifteenth century. These developments quickened the diffusion of knowledge and intellectual exchange, and were able to meet the rising thirst for reading at the universities, at court, and among nobles, bourgeoisie and artisans. By printing the written works of antiquity and making the profane literature of the Greeks and the Romans widely known, scholars made possible the Renaissance and the great developments in the fundamental sciences which were to characterize the seventeenth century.

HOW THE DEVELOPMENT OF MEDIEVAL TECHNOLOGY ENCOURAGED SCIENTIFIC RESEARCH

The development of technology promoted scientific research. The construction of cathedrals posed problems of geometry and statics. While the plans of the thirteenth-century Reims and Strasbourg cathedrals are nothing more than frontal elevations, that of the fourteenth-century cathedral at Siena is lateral; but none as yet is geometrical. The construction of entrapments and catapults required engineers to make certain numerical calculations, though they still fell far short of the ballistics of Galileo and Tartaglia.

Notebooks, such as that of Villard de Honnecourt, show the improvement in research, but it was at Oxford under Robert Grosseteste, Roger Bacon, and Pierre de Maricourt that the scientific spirit founded on experimentation was born.[8] Bacon and Maricourt boasted they had mastered the most diverse arts in order to pierce the secrets of nature. They advocated the inductive method, putting themselves in opposition to the scholastic mentality which relied exclusively on reason and mistrusted the senses. Moreover, they stressed the important role of mathematics in the study of nature.

The new spirit of enterprise also exerted its influence in the realm of science. Commerce with distant continents, geographic studies, banking and financial transactions gave rise to treatises on navigation, accounting, and political economy. These developments were the products of immediate and practical needs, however, rather than the conscious fruit of advances in pure science. Science had to develop on its own through contact with the newly discovered works of the Greek philosophers. Concomitantly, a victory had to be won against what has come to be known as Scholasticism—the bookish teachings of the Church based on the Scriptures and the writings of Aristotle.

Are we justified in talking about a medieval technological revolution? Or is it true, as many affirm, that there were no significant improvements in methods of production between the fifteenth and eighteenth centuries? The developments of this period were numerous: the horse saddle, the shoulder collar for draft animals, the iron horseshoe, the wheelbarrow, the water mill and the windmill, the mechanical saw, the forge with its hammers, glass for windows, the chimney flue, the candle and the wax taper, the wheeled plow with mold-board, the plane, paved streets, the rudder, eyeglasses, mechanical clocks and watches—all of which combined to make life easier and more comfortable.

Despite wars, epidemics, and famines, the peasants' lot improved from century to century. The slave became a serf who could plead in court and, under certain circumstances, marry at will and dispose of his holdings. The serf in turn became a tenant with obligations increasingly expressed in money instead of services. In the cities, artisans and merchants associated themselves in corporations which protected their interests through "just" prices and "fair" wages. If revolts were frequent, this was because serfs were determined to become a part of their societies, economically and socially, and to share in the growing abundance. By the fifteenth century, the cities had become centers of popular civilizations affecting the lives of the people spiritually, artistically, and recreationally. They could no longer be ignored. When science resumed its forward march in the sixteenth and seventeenth centuries, it would be directed toward improving the lot of the common man.

As specialization and trade developed, life tended to become increasingly secular and rational. This tendency is seen in a characteristic publication of the period, the *Practices of Commerce,* which describes commodities, specifies weights and measures, moneys and rates of exchange, tariffs, insurance rates, and shipping routes, and provides formulas for calculating perpetual almanacs. In the fourteenth and fifteenth centuries there were great advances in commercial and financial techniques, such as the beginnings of double-entry bookkeeping, the use of checks and letters of credit, bank deposits and transfers by endorsement, bank money and a more general use of credit, and stock exchanges. In brief, the beginnings of modern capitalism.

These developments turned men's thoughts in new directions, different from those encouraged by the Church. Concern for building an account in heaven and preoccupation with the universal and the supernatural gave way to concern with understanding the realities of present life; the spoken languages of the people began to replace the Latin of the intellectuals. Life ceased to be dominated by liturgy. The religious year started at a date which varied between the 22nd of March and the 25th of April. Traders preferred fixed dates and increasingly opened their accounts on January 1 or July 1. The Church announced the hours and the seasons in accordance with the sun's movements. Merchants found it more convenient to divide the day into twelve or twenty-four equal parts. Automatic clocks sounding the hours replaced the church bells which were rung by hand and regulated by sundials or hourglasses.

The sixteenth century was the century of the Fuggers—a new class of merchants and bankers. They crowned emperors, put popes on the throne of St. Peter's and queens in royal beds. They vied with one another in patronizing artists and embellishing cities, as the cities of Augsburg, Nuremberg, Bruges, Ghent, Genoa, Florence and Venice bear witness. The artist sought new sources of inspiration, different from the Bible and the acts of the martyrs. Ambrogio Lorenzetti decorated the Sala della Pace in the public square of Siena with six allegories portraying good and bad government. A new scale of values was transforming men's ways of thinking, their customs, and their ideas of the universe. A new humanistic spring was following on the long cold winter of the Middle Ages—the Renaissance.

VI

THE RENAISSANCE

In the West, the Middle Ages presents itself to us as a religious civilization dominated by the Church. The great object in life was attainment of personal salvation through the practice of the theological virtues, acceptance of the sacraments and support of the Crusades. The world was but a place of passage, a temporary abode where man prepared himself by penitence for eternity. Sickness, epidemics, famines and natural calamities were manifestations of the divine wrath that man was to accept with resignation. The more troubled man's life, the more meritorious its endurance; death in the sanctity of the faith was the fitting culmination of a virtuous life.

Nature did not exist in and of itself. It was a revelation in which every stone, plant and animal spoke in symbols that man must decipher to understand the puzzle of life and the salutory truths of faith. The task of art, submissive to the decisions of the councils, was to illustrate Holy Writ. The cathedral, its highest expression, was the Bible in stone for simple peasants who could not read. The highest calling was the *vita contemplativa,* to be practiced so far as possible in the solitude of cloister and convent. The queen of the sciences to which all others were subject was theology. In brief, man and creation existed for God, to serve Him and to glorify Him. It was a theocentric civilization.

THE NEW HUMANISM

For this theocentric vision of the world, the Renaissance substituted an entirely new vision which sought to secularize and to a certain extent repaganize life. Existence came to be valued for its own sake. The rewards and punishments which Dante invoked in *The Divine Comedy* and which Orcagna and Fra Angelico depicted on canvas were regarded with skepticism, to be taken seriously only in the throes of death. The great purpose of existence was to live life as vigorously, as agreeably and as luxuriously as possible, and by force of *virtu,* to compose one's existence into a work of art.

The purpose of the plastic arts shifted from the task of illustrating faith to the task of making life more beautiful. Nature ceased to be a vast symbolic abstraction; it existed in its own right, and man's purpose was to analyze its structure, unveil its mysteries, and make it yield its underlying laws through rigorous observation and patient experimentation. In brief, nature was something to be mastered, not simply contemplated. Science thus took on a new importance. Its purpose became the reshaping of the world to the greater comfort of man—a view regarded in the Middle Ages as a sacrilege.

The man of the Renaissance refused to be a subordinated and humiliated creature. In his sculpture and painting he insisted on revealing the plastic beauty of the human body. Botticelli's Venus rose from the waves in triumphant nudity, clothed only in the coils of her golden hair. Leonardo and Vesalius pursued studies of the human body. Engineers and architects confined rivers within new banks, civilized nature, and embellished cities. Historians and economists inquired into the nature of good government. The world ceased to be a vale of tears. Theocentrism, the conception of a world in which man exists only for the service of God, was replaced by humanism, a world in which man exists for himself.

THE REDISCOVERY OF ANCIENT GREECE

This mutation of Western thought was prompted by the rediscovery of Greece. It is to Italy, and particularly to Florence, that we owe this revival. Florence's glory in recapturing what had been lost was hardly less than that of Athens in creating it. Florence revealed Hellenism to the Western world.

Throughout the Middle Ages and as late as the early fifteenth century, copyists who came upon Greek citations in ancient texts would note in the margin *graecum est non ligitur*. Greek was not only a strange language but a fearsome one—the language of heresy. By the latter part of the fifteenth century, all this had changed. In January 1397, Palla Strozzi brought to Florence a Byzantine scholar, Manuel Chrysoloras, who happened to be in Venice on a diplomatic mission. His visit to Florence brought about a miracle; the elite of the city, leaders in government, in the Church, and in business, beardless boys and gray-haired elders flocked to hear him as he opened up to them the glories concealed in the unfamiliar Greek tongue. In three years, Chrysoloras taught Florence to read Greek—to discover Homer, Plato, Thucydides, Xenophon, Polybius, and Demosthenes. Florentines descended upon Byzantium, buying quantities of forgotten texts; clerks combed the monasteries of Italy, Switzerland, and Germany for Greek and Latin texts that had escaped the great burning which marked Rome's embrace of Christianity and the great invasion.

Cosimo de' Medici (1389–1464) put an army of copyists to work and gave generously to the library of St. Marks and the abbey at Fiesole, and opened his own magnificent library in the Riccardi Palace to professors and students. He and his grandson, Lorenzo the Magnificent (1449–92), gathered around themselves an army of scholars and translators. Before the century was over, if we may believe Politian, the children of the nobility spoke Greek so fluently and idiomatically that "one could easily believe that Athens had not been destroyed and occupied by the barbarians, but rather had been moved to Florence, bag and baggage, and that Florence had completely and totally absorbed her." [1]

In Florence the East and West met and fused. The ecumenical council of 1439 which embodied this union is marvelously evoked by the brush of Benozzo Gozzoli (1420–97) on the walls of the chapel of the Riccardi Palace, where we see John Paleologus, the patriarch of Constantinople and the emperor of the Orient, in his costume of gold brocade at the head of the procession of the wise men. With the discovery of Hellenism, the gentle breeze of tolerance once again stirred on the peninsula. The churchmen of the West entered the council not as if they were meeting with schismatics and renegades, but in the spirit of meeting with the authentic descendants of Homer, Plato, and Demosthenes. At the Church of Santa Maria Novella, two thrones of equal eminence were erected, one for the pope of Rome and the other for the emperor of the East.

PLATO IN FLORENCE

Italian humanism replaced the Scholasticism which had so long held sway; the divine Plato, called by the Schoolmen "the evangelical doctor," replaced Aristotle. The elder Cosimo was reading one of Plato's dialogues at the moment of his death. Lorenzo de' Medici was certain that without the Platonic discipline, one could not be a good citizen, or a good Christian. Marsilio Ficino preached Platonism [2] from his pulpit; Plato was to him the Attic Moses. When Raphael depicted the Dispute of the Holy Sacrament School at Athens and Parnassus in the Hall of the Signatures in the Vatican, it was the composite Platonic religion of the Florentines that he immortalized.

THE UNIVERSAL MAN

From the study of antiquity emerged a new ideal of man. It was a denial of the medieval ideal of a man with only a single activity, specialized and neatly fitted into a hierarchical structure. The new passion for understanding, the need to create, and the Renaissance exuberance for life disregarded customary classifications and broke through all social barriers to create the universal man, the man who embodied the culture of his age and mastered all the arts and sciences. Brunelleschi (1377–1446) knew all the disciplines relative to architecture and applied mathematical calculations to the design of the cupola of the Dome; he was a sculptor as well, expressing his talents as widely as did Michelangelo. The curiosity of Leonardo da Vinci knew no bounds. The man of the Renaissance was a man for whom nothing was forbidden, who abandoned the idea of original sin, who admired above all intellectual and moral daring, who valued aesthetics more than ethics, and who was at home in any surroundings. Like Dante in exile, he could say, "My country is the whole world."

THE GOLDEN AGE OF THE MEDICI

Never did a small city give the world in so short a time such a galaxy of artists. Through the rivalry of wealthy patrons and of the corporations of craftsmen and merchants, this ancient and somber city of communal quarrels was transformed into a thing of beauty. Under Lorenzo the Magnificent, life in Florence took on the appearance of a perpetual fair. On the slopes, among the olive trees, the cypresses, and the rose bushes, and in the villas of the Medici, members of the academy founded by Cosimo de' Medici met and engaged in the same brilliant discussions that had marked the Athens of Pericles and the Rome of Augustus. This, as a contemporary saw it, was a golden age "which had revived at almost the moment of their final death the great liberal disciplines: grammar, poetry, eloquence, painting, architecture, sculpture, music and the art of singing to the lyre of Orpheus . . ." [3]

THE SPREAD OF THE RENAISSANCE

The Florence of the Medici collapsed under the blows of the theocratic demagogue, Savonarola. When Savonarola struck at riches, he struck at the very foundations of the city, which had become a center of industry and Europe's banker, precisely because it was a community in which men were free. In exorcising the Renaissance and bringing back the dark spirit of the Middle Ages, this quixotic friar ruined beyond repair the city's banks and crafts. But the spirit of Florence spread as bees do at swarming time, finding new hives at Milan, Mantua, Verona, Venice, Rimini, Naples, and in the Rome of the Humanistic popes. The same spirit spread to France, the Low Countries, Germany, England, Bohemia, and Poland.

Florentine humanism eventually became pedantic and academic, but in its search for Greek books, in its zeal to get them translated and published, it made its great contribution. It served as schoolmaster to all Europe; everywhere its pupils would found libraries and academies where Greek and Oriental languages would be taught—the Greek academy at Rome and the College of France in Paris being but two examples.

THE SECULARIZATION OF LIFE

This rediscovery by the humanists of the Greek and Latin civilizations, which for more than a thousand years had occupied the highest reaches of science, philosophy, literature, and art without any traces of Judaism and Christianity, had an even more profound effect on men's minds than the great geographic discoveries which were occurring simultaneously. Comparisons were made between the Trojan wars in Homer's *Iliad* and the wars of Jahweh, between the sages of Greece and the prophets of Israel, between Pythagoras, Socrates, and Plato, and the Fathers of the Church, and the comparisons turned in favor of the pagans. A civilization had existed where men had not even heard of Moses or of Christ, where men were ignorant of original sin and the threat of hell, and yet did not throw anathemas at a fallen and corrupted nature but rather followed it as a counselor and teacher. A civilization had existed where rituals were separated from beliefs, intelligence was not humiliated before faith, and the passion to know was not regarded as perilous lust. Contact with the liberty of spirit which the philosophers of Greece enjoyed, the art of living of the Periclean and Augustinian ages swept away the Christian code of humility, continence, and renunciation, and liberated an exuberance for life which had been too long suppressed.

The people of Italy became the most skeptical of Europeans; Pomponazzi, Aretino, Leonardo da Vinci, Machiavelli and Cellini were either frank atheists or completely indifferent to religion. High dignitaries of state viewed religion as a salutary myth to answer the need for wonder in the souls of the simple and to exhort the poor to be patient in adversity. Everything invited incredulity—the defeat of the Crusades, the exile at Avignon, the scandals of the schism, the immorality and worldliness of the clergy, popes more concerned for temporal power than for the poor, and for pomp and ceremony than for their spiritual responsibilities and the wounds of Christ. The traffic in indulgences, nepotism, the sale of red hats, all went to provoke the Reformation and the Counter-Reformation.

Under the influence of the new spirit, of the development of wealth, of the independent authority of artists, of the resistance in commercial and financial circles to ecclesiastical domination, life was secularized. The Reformation and Counter-Reformation and the wave of intolerance and violence which they provoked destroyed part of the influence of the Renaissance; but throughout the seventeenth century the Renaissance spirit would not be silenced, and it rose again in the French "century of light."

THE GREAT DISCOVERIES

The century that witnessed the rediscovery of Greek culture saw also the discovery of the New World. The Middle Ages had a very restricted knowledge of the globe, and the cult of ignorance, the *ama nescire,* was not calculated to stimulate inquiry. Lactantius, the teacher of the son of Constantine, taught his pupil that ignorance of geography was agreeable to the Lord. During these long centuries, it was the barbarians on the periphery of Europe who embarked on voyages of discovery. The long boats of the Vikings sailed to Ireland, Greenland, crossed Davis Strait, and approached Vineland. The caravans of the Arabs penetrated into the interior of Africa and the interminable deserts of central Asia.

The obligation which Jesus laid upon his Disciples to convert the peoples of the earth, joined to the incitements to trade at the time of the Fuggers and Medicis, did, however, stimulate some exploratory zeal. The Crusades, the voyages of the Venetians to China, the caravels of Christ launched by Henry the Navigator to establish trading posts in the land of spices, the discovery of America by Columbus and Amerigo Vespucci, revealed continents which had been undreamed of. The voyagers uncovered flora and fauna so numerous that men asked themselves how all these new species could have fitted into Noah's ark, and brought to light races of which there was no mention in the Bible, beings so strange that the theologians of Salamanca wondered if they were to be treated as men or as beasts to be exploited. Marco Polo found at the court of the Grand Khan a civilization much more advanced than any known to Europe. It was apparent that Christianity was only the religion of one small continent in the midst of an enormous world where countless other religions were professed.

One of the greatest spiritual ambassadors of Christianity, the Franciscan André of Perusia, wrote about China to the venerable abbot of the monastery at Perusia in the winter of 1330: "in this immense empire there exist peoples belonging to all races to be found under the sun, and men of all confessions. All have the right to live according to their beliefs. One thinks here, presumably incorrectly, that everyone can be happy in his own religion." [4]

The Bible and the encyclopedias of the Middle Ages had concealed many things. Other civilizations, far superior to medieval Latin Christendom, had existed and prospered. Other religions than Christianity had illuminated and consoled the sorrowful existence of men. All the accepted certitudes were shaken. But thanks to Copernicus, Kepler, Galileo, and Newton, a revelation much more surprising was yet to come. These scientists would substitute for the closed and finite world of antiquity and the Middle Ages the open and infinite world of modern times.

VII

THE SCIENTIFIC REVOLUTION

The technical inventions of the Middle Ages had for the most part put to practical use the amusing creations of the engineers of the school of Alexandria. They were the result of empiricism rather than of theoretical science.

THE REDISCOVERY OF THE SCIENTIFIC
WORKS OF ANTIQUITY

The Renaissance and the accompanying contact with the re-discovered scholarship of the Greeks were to bring about a radical change. The triumph of Christianity in the West as the religion of the state had provoked one of the greatest destructions of books, manuscripts, libraries and works of art ever recorded in history. If a few works survived this holocaust, it was due to some old Romans, high dignitaries of the court of Theodoric. It is not to the West, but to the Orient—Byzantium, Syria, Persia and Arabia—that we owe the survival of Hellenic culture.

Between the thirteenth and sixteenth centuries the works of Archimedes, Apollonius, and others reached the West via Syria, Baghdad, Cordova, Toledo, and Palermo, arousing scientific thought from its long sleep. It was a passage in Archimedes which led Copernicus to the hypothesis of the heliocentric universe; it was Apollonius who led Kepler to substitute an ellipse for a circle in his explanation of the orbits of the planets; and above all, it was Archimedes who taught Leonardo da Vinci, Benedetti and Galileo to use mathematics in their studies of nature. A problem posed by Pappus on the locus of points led Descartes to create analytical geometry. There are many such examples. It is not too great a claim to say that the fate of Western civilization turned on the almost haphazard preservation of a few dozen ancient manuscripts.

THE REAWAKENING OF THE SCIENTIFIC SPIRIT
THE INSISTENCE THAT IT BE USEFUL

The discovery of the writings of these Greek scientists, especially those of Archimedes, reawakened the scientific spirit, the passion for knowledge which the Fathers of the Church, the mystics, and the learned Schoolmen of the Middle Ages had condemned as sinful curiosity.

Science resumed its upward flight but with an added motive unknown to the ancients: that it be useful, that it be directed to the practical needs of men, and that it reduce the pain and toil of life. It thus ceased to be a purely speculative pursuit; it became active and functional. It took on a social significance. Almost overnight the mechanical arts, so despised by the ancients, were rehabilitated and glorified.

Leonardo da Vinci was an engineer as well as a pure scientist. His attitude toward the speculations of the Schoolmen is representative of the new men of the Renaissance: "If we were to believe them, knowledge derived from experimentation is purely mechanical, while that which is born of the spirit and ends in the spirit is alone scientific." [1] He insisted that knowledge which did not rest on experimentation was apt to be "vain and full of error" and that, as a consequence, "mechanical and instrumental science is the most noble and elevates itself above all others because of its utility." [2] Whereas Aristotle had unfavorably compared the stagnation

of the mechanical arts with the progress made in the speculative sciences in his time, Francis Bacon said the opposite was
true, that for centuries past there had been no perceptible
progress in the field of philosophical speculation whereas
progress in the mechanical arts had transformed the world,
and that men should therefore study these arts even though
they seemed illiberal. Descartes denied value to anything or
any idea which was of no use to anyone.

THE GIANTS OF THE RENAISSANCE

Leonardo da Vinci

Space prevents us from doing more than a sketch of a few
traits of four of the great giants of the Renaissance: Leonardo da Vinci, Francis Bacon, Galileo, and Descartes.

Leonardo da Vinci (1452–1519), painter, sculptor, architect,
engineer, and scientist, was the very embodiment of the Renaissance. The Middle Ages had regarded nature as a mirror
which reflected the image of revealed truths. It was an imag-
inary Bible, and the greatest feat of learning was to decipher
its symbolism. Leonardo, on the contrary, insisted that nature
be studied for its own sake. He scrutinized its mysteries,
analyzed its structures, dissected its mechanisms, and sought
to discover its laws. He rejected the authority of the ancients
—above all Aristotle's. "Who cites authority to support his
case gives proof, not of great talent, but of an excellent
memory." [3] He denounced the humanists as puffed-up· and
pompous, and they in turn called him illiterate. "They fail
to realize that my works have to meet the test of experience
and not just the dictum of other men, and that experience is
the mother of all whose writing can be trusted." [4]

For Leonardo, experience was the source of reliable knowledge. "It never deceives us; it is our judgment that leads us

into error, because it looks for effects which are denied to it by experimentation." What was needed, he continued, was a multiplication of experiments, "in order to see whether the same experiments always produce the same effects." [5] In order to state the laws of nature in mathematical form, he maintained, it was necessary to construct measuring instruments, and he devised many: the dynometer, the hydrometer and the odometer.

Leonardo also created a screw propeller, paddle wheels, agricultural machines that could be moved by the wind, a variety of vehicles, a clock, machines for rolling iron, twisting cord, carding, polishing, digging ditches, and making cylinders, saws, vises, and files. He invented mechanical presses, boring machines, hammers for beating gold, faucets for hot and cold water, and lamps with double air vents. As a military engineer he designed the machine gun, cannons fired by hot gases, portable bridges, field mines, bombs, tanks, submarines, and flying machines. At the same time, he concealed many of these discoveries, as Tartaglia was to do, fearing that the malignity of man would put them to bad use. Stigmatizing war as "the most bestial folly," for "it is a terrible thing to take the life of a man," he admitted that if men were all virtuous, he would devote himself to teaching them to fly. If he imagined means of offense and defense, it was always in order to make them serve "the preservation of the principal gift of nature: liberty." [6]

His work *Quaderni d'Anatomia* put him in the front rank of anatomists. He identified the ventricles of the brain and of the heart. He was a physiologist; he knew that the blood circulates; he studied reflex movements and made experiments on the spinal cord of the frog, anticipating the work of Vesalius and Harvey. He was the father of paleontology; he recognized, half a century before Palissy, that fossils found in rocks and alluvial soils give us knowledge of the natural history of the earth. He was interested in the strength of materials, in hydraulics, aerodynamics, meteorology, optics, acoustics, and astronomy. He explored all the avenues of knowledge, and wherever he traveled he was master.

But science, to Leonardo, could not be simply empirical and descriptive. It had also to be theoretical, for otherwise it would be disorganized and blind. It also had to be capable of mathematical formulation. The concept of science developed by Leonardo is the one that prevails today. He anticipated a number of basic principles, such as the principle of least action, of inertia, of statics and the physics of solids and fluids. As early as 1508, when Copernicus had only begun to meditate on the system of the world, Leonardo asserted that the earth did not occupy the center of the universe and was not the center of the orbit of the sun. He was one of the first men of the modern era by virtue of his rejection of the ancient prohibitions, of his effort to understand everything, and of his confidence that science and its applications could improve the human condition. "To live," he wrote, "is to understand. I will cease to be alive before I will cease to want to be useful. I shall die before I know the meaning of lassitude." And again he wrote, "Just as the well-spent day deserves a happy sleep, so a well-employed life assures us of a happy death." [7]

Francis Bacon

Bacon (1561–1626) proposed to revive and extend knowledge by combining theory and practice (craftsmanship). Traditional scholarship, he argued, had lost contact with experience, while practice, largely unwritten, was ineffectual because purely empirical. A union of the two would produce inventions capable of reducing the misery of mankind. The world would have been none the worse off had Aristotle's books been burned. They contained nothing capable of serving the well-being of men.[8] The purpose and justification of knowledge was human welfare, "the endowment of human life with inventions and wealth." [9] Science was a tool, an *organum,* which permitted the human spirit to understand and to master the forces of nature.

While Bacon was not the founder of the scientific method, he was the first to insist upon the importance of induction—this though he was not an expert practitioner (his knowledge of mathematics was insufficient). His conception of the scientific method remained essentially qualitative and inductive.

New Atlantis, Bacon's contribution to utopian literature, is significant for its astounding anticipation of future scientific developments. A storm has tossed some travelers onto the uncharted island of Bensalem. This island is the domain of scientific research. Bacon describes the vast array of equipment used to study the secrets of the generation of minerals, the effects of heat, meteors, the nature of the air and of the sun. He imagined great rooms whose climates could be controlled, baths, agricultural experiments, dissecting rooms, clinics, physical laboratories, mathematical institutes, observatories, lighter-than-air balloons, submarines, the transformation of animal and vegetable species, conservation of foods, and discoveries of many remedies.

The whole thing would be directed by a college of specialists, the president of which declares: "The purpose of our institute is the discovery of causes and of intimate knowledge of the primordial forces and principles of things, in order to expand the limits of the control of man over nature and in order to achieve everything that is possible." [10]

Galileo Galilei

Galileo (1564–1642) may be regarded as the founder of modern science. He created and practiced the scientific method, as the term is understood today. He provided the definitive refutation of the physics of Aristotle and founded modern dynamics. He proved the physical reality of helio-centrism, something which thitherto had been admitted only as a convenient mathematical fiction, and thus revealed the infinite world which so excited Giordano Bruno and fright-ened Blaise Pascal. And finally, he secularized the natural sciences by freeing them from the double yoke of Aristotle and the Scriptures.

The scientific method does not stop with passively record-ing the testimony of the senses but goes on to break up the elements involved in perception and to isolate them one by one in their proper context, sometimes with the aid of purely mental operations, and sometimes with the aid of precision instruments such as Galileo himself invented: the telescope, microscope, geometric compass, hydrostatic scales, thermo-scope, thermometer, and the pendulum clock which Huygens would later improve.

Aristotle had taught that the earth was the center of a universe encompassed by the enveloping sphere of the fixed stars. Galileo destroyed this comforting picture. He showed that there is a single universe filled with stars which them-selves are centers of attraction, and that our earth is but one body among a multiplicity of others. One could no longer consider the earth the center of the universe. In mechanics he discovered the principle of inertia; he formulated the laws of falling bodies and anticipated the infinitesimal calculus, thus making it possible for Newton to show that a single prin-ciple can account for the motions of both celestial and earthly bodies. Galileo presaged later astrophysics with his under-standing of the substantial unity of the world, and thus echoed after more than twenty centuries the monism of the first Ionian physicists.

René Descartes

Descartes's (1596–1650) original intention was to entitle his famous *Discourse on Method* (1637) "A Project for a Universal Science Capable of Elevating Our Natures to the Highest Degree of Perfection." Here we see the idea of the perfectibility of nature which will be one of the motive forces of the Enlightenment. In the *Discourse* he proposed a "practical philosophy, through which, by understanding the force and action of fire, water, air, the stars, the heavens and all the other bodies surrounding us as well as we understand the diverse trades of our artisans, we could employ these forces in an enlightened manner and thereby become the very masters and possessors of nature." [11] No longer was it enough to know the world; it must be changed.

Descartes eliminated the physics of final causes, of substantial forms and occult qualities. His model of the universe was as simple as a piece of clockwork and answered the need of practical men for an explanation of things. The search for a mechanical explanation of all phenomena was to become the major preoccupation of physicists and would lead to some magnificent discoveries, such as the atomic theory, the kinetic theory, the theory of gases, the mechanical theory of sound, which would prevail until replaced in our own times by quantum theory and relativity. His contributions to method in the fields of biology, chemistry, and physiology were equally significant.

By insisting upon accepting as true only what seemed self-evident and by making the principles of free inquiry the first requirement of his method, Descartes in effect wrote the charter for the great revolution which would assert the right to criticize every belief and every tradition which justified itself by an appeal to authority. He tried, unsuccessfully, to exempt religion and the political institutions of France from the exercise of his method. The critical spirit of the eighteenth century would demand an accounting from every institution and every custom, be it economic, political or moral.

The *Discourse* was written in French, not Latin, thus inviting people of all classes–peasants, artisans, burghers and gentry, men and women–to join a free parliament, an immense assembly of thinking men.

THE AGE OF ACADEMIES BEGINS

The requirements of technical education, coming as they did with the development of the fundamental sciences, are reflected in the many learned societies which made their appearance in the sixteenth and seventeenth centuries. The first were in Italy: the Accadèmia Secretorum Naturae at Naples (ca. 1560); the Accadèmia del Cimento at Florence (ca. 1567); the Accadèmia del Lincei at Rome (ca. 1601). The British Royal Society "to promote the knowledge of nature and the improvement of the useful arts" was founded in 1662. The French minister Colbert sponsored an Academie des sciences four years later. Toward the end of the eighteenth century there were no less than thirty-seven important provincial academies in France. In Germany, due to the efforts of Leibnitz, the Berlin Academy opened in 1700, and in 1724 St. Petersburg had its one academy.[12]

VIII

THE CONFLICT BETWEEN
THEOLOGY AND SCIENCE

The scientific spirit had been finally aroused from its long slumber. Before it could exert its full effect, however, a handicap as damaging to the spirit of the West as slavery had been to Greco-Roman civilization had to be removed. A double victory had to be won against the authority of the Church and the authority of Aristotle. Timid signs of restlessness had appeared as early as the fourteenth century among the Parisian nominalists, but the scientific spirit fully affirmed itself beginning with the Italian Renaissance in the sixteenth century and extending throughout Europe in the seventeenth.

THE CONFLICT BETWEEN THE BIBLE AND THE SCIENTIFIC SPIRIT

Primitive Christianity appeared at first as one of the Oriental religions of salvation which Alexander's conquests had spread throughout the western Mediterranean. In place of science and of the disinterested search for truth it substituted gnosis, or a belief in revelation transcending human reason, such as the mystery of the cross, preached by Paul, concealed from even the wisest of sages.

The whole hierarchy of values of the Greco-Roman world was turned upside down. Faith was more important than knowledge. In the words of Paul, "For the wisdom of the world is folly with God." [1] And two hundred years later Tertullian (d. ca. 230 A.D.), the Roman theologian, asked what Athens (logic) had to do with Jerusalem (faith). "What concord is there between the Academy and the Church?" [2]

For the Fathers of the Church, for the doctors of the Middle Ages, and for the great preachers of the classical age, the passion for knowledge—*libido sciendi*—which Plato and Aristotle had regarded as the supreme accomplishment of human life, was considered as damning as the other passions. Paul declared, "Knowledge puffs up, but love builds up." [3] Augustine wrote, "God and the soul—is there anything more? No, nothing!" He scoffed at the astronomers who study the passage of the stars across the skies and "are ignorant of our Father who is in heaven." [4] Pierre Duhem observes:

For the Fathers of the Church, research into physics and astronomy are futile and idle occupations; if they content themselves, begrudgingly, to pay attention to these researches, it is solely with an eye to interpreting Holy Scripture and to countering the objections of the pagan philosophers against the Bible.[5]

Throughout the Middle Ages and into modern times, this attitude, this *ama nescire* (love of ignorance) would persist. Even Pascal (d. 1662), after his conversion, would reproach Descartes and Copernicus for delving too deeply into sciences which, even were they true, would not be "worth one hour of pain." [6]

If Christianity had limited itself to discouraging scientific research as a useless diversion (to use the language of Pascal), it would have been bad enough; but it went much further than that. It undertook to stop such research as a threat to faith. Once the canon of Holy Scripture and the ecclesiastical hierarchy had been established, the hierarchy demanded that it alone be the interpreter of religious meaning. Acceptance of the dogmas, as defined by the fathers and the councils, became an essential condition of salvation, counting more than the observation of the moral law and the practice of charity. "Whoever wishes to be saved must above all else keep the Catholic faith. If he does not conserve it in its entirety and inviolate, his eternal damnation is certain." [7]

Now the Bible, and the dogmas drawn from it, were bound to an impossible physics, to an archaic world view, to an embarrassing biology and anthropology, and to a mythical and apocalyptic interpretation of history. Consequently, every discovery in every domain ran up against a citation from Scripture and for that alone was condemned. Had not Augustine declared that "nothing should be accepted, save on the authority of the Bible, for this authority is much greater than the capacity of the human spirit"? And had he not demonstrated that the earth could not be round from the fact that "on the day of judgment those who would be on the other side of the world would not be able to see the Lord descend from the clouds"? [8] Thus began the long and painful conflict between science and theology.

Profane science, insofar as it was tolerated at all, was entirely bookish. It was thought to be contained in the Ptolemaic astronomy, in the natural science of Aristotle and in the medicine of Galen. All experimental research which departed from these authorities was suspected of magic, of "illegitimate traffic with the devil." Alchemy, the forerunner of modern chemistry, was ranked as one of the "seven deadly sciences" because it sought to create new elements. The greatest researchers of the Middle Ages were all suspected of being in league with the devil. Roger Bacon, banished from Oxford in 1257 for insisting on the need for experimentation, was eventually imprisoned for fourteen years "for certain novelties of a suspicious nature." [9] Vesalius, the father of scientific anatomy, was harassed by the Inquisition, and Servetus, the discoverer of the principles of respiration, was condemned to the stake by Calvin. Whoever affirmed a new idea risked being accused of heresy.

THE CONFLICT BETWEEN ARISTOTLE AND THE SCIENTIFIC SPIRIT

The conflict between science and theology went hand in hand with another conflict, that between science and Aristotle.

When Christianity penetrated the skeptical and cultivated levels of pagan society, its defenders felt the need of proving it could be upheld not only by the Hebraic method, "by prophets and miracles," but also by the Hellenic method, "by dialectic." They undertook to prove the rationality of their faith by showing the consistency of its revelations with the wisdom of the pagan philosophers who were to the Gentiles what the prophets were to the Jews. They argued, for example, that the philosophers had either plagiarized Holy Scriptures or, more charitably, been inspired by the same divine Spirit. Plato thus came to be regarded as a Moses in Greek dress.

A major problem for the Scholastics was the reconciliation of faith and reason—faith as found in the Church's interpretations of revelation, and reason as found in the writings of the pagan philosophers, particularly the works of Aristotle, which had become known in the Latin West for the first time in their entirety in the thirteenth century. These works were regarded as containing the sum total of the knowledge which the human mind was capable of acquiring through its own efforts.

Of all the philosophical systems of antiquity, Aristotle's was at once the most compatible and the most incompatible with the Christian faith. It was the most compatible because the world of Aristotle fitted marvelously into the topography of Holy Scriptures. Aristotle differentiated sharply between the heavenly realm of the moon and the fixed stars, incorruptible and unchanging, and the sublunary world within the orbit of the moon and composed of an unstable mixture of four elements: earth, air, fire, and water, ever changing and liable to corruption and death. Only slight changes in this system were needed to Christianize it, to reconcile it with the account of the Creation in the Book of Genesis, or with the account in Paul's Second Letter to the Corinthians of the man who had been carried to the third heaven.[10] In Genesis, God separated the celestial waters from the terrestrial by the firmament. The Fathers of the Church superimposed upon the sky of the fixed stars a crystalline sky enclosing the celestial waters, above these was the Empyrean, or third, Heaven, the realm of the Trinity and the Blessed. Such was the salutary image of the world derived from a Christianized Aristotle, which Dante used in his *Divine Comedy*.

Yet, among all the systems of antiquity, the metaphysics of Aristotle appeared most incompatible with Christianity. The Unmoved Mover of Aristotle moved the sky of the fixed stars, drew from matter its ordained forms by the power of attraction, and utterly ignored the eternally existing world. This doctrine negated the Creation, Providence, the possibility of miracles and grace, to which must be added the negation of the immortality of the soul and the idea of rewards and punishments in an afterlife. When the entire works of Aristotle became known to the West in the thirteenth century, the first reaction of ecclesiastical authority was to ban them.

The attraction of Aristotle was, however, irresistible. Very wisely the Church decided that it would be better to attempt a reconciliation. Thomas Aquinas (d. 1274) undertook the task. To succeed, Aquinas had to transform a purely logical distinction of Aristotle into a real one. This enabled him to prove the necessity for the Creator, the contingency of the Creation, and the possibility of the dogmas of the Incarnation, the Trinity and the Eucharist. But in so doing, Aquinas disrupted the entire harmony of the Aristotelian system. If one rejects the *real* distinction between essence and existence, one can no longer justify by reason the foundations of faith, or prove that the dogmas of Incarnation, Trinity, and Eucharist are not antirational, only superrational.

Duns Scotus (d. 1308) rejected Aquinas's proofs for the existence of God. God's will being completely free, we cannot formulate any law concerning the fashion in which He exercises it. A ditch was dug between faith and reason. The gulf became complete when William of Occam (d. ca. 1349) promulgated a pure nominalism, according to which only individual and particular things can be the objects of experience. On that basis one is unable to prove the existence of God, His attributes, or the spirituality and immortality of the soul. Nor can one show the noncontradiction of the dogmas of the Church. These beliefs depend on faith; answers to the great questions of metaphysics all involve some doubtful affirmation or some proposition taken on faith. Averroists managed to escape this position by holding a theory of double truth: a proposition can be true in philosophy and the contrary proposition can still be true in theology, because God can choose to act according to the ways of nature, to the philosophy of Aristotle, or to supernatural ways.

Occamism ends up in a pure declaration of faith. It put a final end to Scholasticism by denying the possibility of rational theology. The foundations of faith were transferred from the domain of natural philosophy to the domain of positive theology, based on the authority of the Scriptures, the Fathers, and the councils. Philosophy is reduced to logic and physics, but in ceasing to be the servant of theology it gained its autonomy. In spite of the ecclesiastical condemnations heaped upon it, Occamism, after being developed at Oxford, implanted itself in the University of Paris, where throughout the fourteenth and part of the fifteenth century it favored the awakening of scientific thought by emancipating it from theology and from Aristotle.

Thomas Aquinas had attempted to create a harmony between Aristotle and dogma. He failed, but his effort introduced reason, like a Trojan horse, into the citadel of faith.
His effort to rationalize dogma was an implicit recognition
of the authority of reason. Introduced as the servant of
theology, reason was soon to become the master. The more
violent the disputes among the doctors, the theologians, the
schools and sects, the more reason was invoked by one group
against the other, and the more reason saw her empire and
authority grow.

THE FOUR CRITERIA OF TRUTH

The victory of reason might have been won in the fourteenth
and fifteenth centuries had it not been for the Reformation
and Counter-Reformation. These movements led the Church
to insist once more upon the authority of the Scriptures and
of Aristotle.

The Counter-Reformation broke the tacit agreement established during the Renaissance between the Church and the
humanists. The Fifth Lateran Council (1512–17) required
prior ecclesiastical approval before any book could be published, and in 1555 enforcement was turned over to the Inquisition. Under the fanatical Paul IV, who had boasted that
if his own father were a heretic he would gather the faggots
with which to burn him, enforcement became severe. The
dread Index, to quote the verdict of Paolo Sarpi, a friend of
Galileo, became "the most perfect device ever discovered for
reducing man to the level of the beasts." [11] The Protestant
sects showed themselves no less fanatical.

Thus at the beginning of the seventeenth century, a physical theory had to meet four conditions to be acceptable to
the Church: it had to be coherent, it had to agree with the
physics of Aristotle, it had to be compatible with the letter of
Scripture, and, according to an ancient formula, it had "to

save the appearances"—to agree with the testimony of the senses.

THE INCOMPATIBILITY BETWEEN SCRIPTURE, ARISTOTLE AND THE COPERNICAN SYSTEM

Numerous theories of the universe were in circulation. One scholar listed seventy-nine. Copernicus revived one attributed to Aristarchus of Samos (d. ca. 270 B.C.), which held that the earth and other planets circulated around the sun, which was immobile and formed the center of the universe. Copernicus developed this heliocentric theory and set it forth with supporting arguments in his *On the Revolutions of Celestial Bodies.*

The conclusions were so clearly at variance with the physics of Aristotle and certain passages in the Bible that Copernicus was seriously tempted to burn the manuscript. Friends protested and he finally gave in and allowed it to be published in what was to be the last year of his life (1543), with a dedication to Pope Paul III which he hoped would protect him.

A scandal was only avoided by a subterfuge perpetrated by Andreas Osiander, charged with supervising the publishing of the book. He substituted a preface which the dying author did not see, in which the Copernican system was presented as a mathematical fiction useful because it simplified the calculations needed to construct an almanac. He wrote: "The author of this work has written nothing which merits blame. It is not necessary that his hypotheses be true, or even reasonable. Only one thing is required, that they offer a method of calculation corresponding to observations . . . Astronomy chooses by preference the hypothesis which is most simple. Philosophy will perhaps demand more verisimilitude. But without the aid of divine revelation neither the one nor the other can discover or teach anything which is certain." [12] The final word remained with the theologians.

Presented simply as a mathematical fiction, the heliocentric system might satisfy the ecclesiastical authorities. It would be an entirely different matter if it were presented as a physical reality, and this is exactly what Kepler (d. 1630) and Galileo (d. 1642) would do. And Luther, it should be noted, would not accept even as a fiction the contentions of "this fool who wished to turn upside down the entire art of astronomy."

Kepler proved that the planets did not follow a uniform movement in their orbits but rather described ellipses with the sun occupying one of the foci, and thus made a shambles of the whole Aristotelian celestial mechanics. Galileo went even further. With the aid of his powerful telescope, he discovered the satellites of Jupiter, the rings of Saturn, the terrestrial-like surface of the moon, and spots on the sun; he proved that the Milky Way is a collection of celestial bodies independent of our solar system. In place of the finite universe of Aristotle, Galileo substituted a universe of infinite space. With the discoveries he reported to his contemporaries in *Siderus Nuncius* (1610), the human soul changed dimensions.

From this time forward, the conflict between Galileo, the Aristotelians and the theologians was inevitable.

THE LETTER OF GALILEO TO THE GRAND DUCHESS OF TUSCANY

Attacked by the Lutheran Church, Kepler's defense had been: "If it is a question of faith and conduct, one should consult the Scriptures; if it is a question of astronomy and physics one should consult the book of nature. In theology, one weighs authorities, in philosophy, the reason of things." [13]

Galileo responded in similar vein in a letter which he addressed to the grand duchess of Tuscany, the grandmother of the reigning duke:

In any discussion of problems of physics one should not take as his authorities sacred books, but experiments and demonstrations. In effect the Scriptures and Nature both proceed from the same divine Word: the one, as dictated by the Holy Spirit, and the other, as the obedient executor of God's orders. But, while the Scriptures, adapting themselves to the intelligence of the average man, must speak frequently in visual images, and in terms which, if taken literally, are at variance with the truth; nature, on the other hand, conforms inexorably and unfailingly to the laws imposed upon it without ever exceeding their limits, and is not concerned whether its concealed reasons and methods of operation are capable of being understood by men. From this it follows that we should not doubt or deny natural phenomena revealed to our eyes or proved by necessary conclusions, and even less should we condemn them in the name of passages from the Bible whose literal meaning would seem to contradict them. For the words of the Bible are not subject to restraints as imperious as the effects of nature are, and God does not less admirably reveal Himself in the actions of nature than in the sacred words of the Bible.

To prohibit at this time the Copernican system, when a multiplicity of new observations confirm it more decisively each day and when this book is steadily becoming better known among men of letters, especially after having tolerated it for many years when it was less well known and less certain, would be, in my opinion, to put oneself in opposition to truth . . . Certainly, on all propositions which are not directly dependent on the faith, no doubt the sovereign Pontiff has the absolute power in any case to approve or condemn them; but it is not within the power of any creature to render them true or false, and other than they are in nature and in fact.[14]

In thus maintaining that the Scriptures were authoritative only in faith and morals, and not in physical matters, so that in case of a conflict between them the Scriptures should be interpreted allegorically, Galileo thought he had disarmed his adversaries. On the contrary, he had signed his own condemnation.

THE TRIAL OF GALILEO

On the 5th of March, 1616, the Congregation of the Index published the decree suspending Copernicus's book, *The Revolution of the Celestial Globe,* until it could be corrected, and at the same forbade and suspended all other works which set forth Copernican doctrine. Exactly sixteen years later, Galileo published his *Dialogue on Two Chief Systems of the World* with an imprimatur painfully obtained after two years of negotiations. Although the two systems—that of Copernicus and that of Ptolemy—were presented as hypotheses, the new pope, Urban VIII, was persuaded by the Jesuits that he had been personally attacked and ridiculed through the character of Simplicius, defender of the Ptolemaic system, and that the *Dialogue* was "more damnable and more of a threat to the Holy Church than the writings of Calvin and Luther." [15]

Procedures against Galileo were inevitable, and the sentence of the Holy Office was read on the morning of June 22 in the great hall of the Dominican convent of Santa Maria to Galileo, on his knees in the shirt of a penitent:

The proposition that the sun is the center of the universe and immovable *is absurd and false in philosophy and clearly heretical, as it is clearly contrary to Holy Scripture.* The proposition that the earth is neither the center of the universe nor immobile, but moves, and moreover that it moves in a daily motion, is equally a *proposition which is absurd and false in philosophy, and considered in theology at the very least erroneous according to the faith.*[16]

Thereafter the book was prohibited and its author, strongly suspected of heresy, was condemned to the prison of the Holy Office, a sentence commuted to perpetual confinement to his house near Florence. The Holy Office sent to all the nuncios of Europe, to the archbishops and bishops, and to the inquisition in Italy copies of the sentence pronounced against Galileo, as well as copies of his recantation, with orders to make them known to all parish curates.

Despite all this, Galileo's spirit was not broken. In his confinement he composed between 1633 and 1637 his masterpiece, the *Dialogue on Two New Sciences,* which was destined to establish modern dynamics. A few months before his death he was busy devising a clock with a balance wheel. And almost a year before his death, sick and blind, he dictated a letter full of irony to the Aristotelian, Fortuno Luceti:

If all that is true in philosophy were contained in Aristotle you would, in my opinion, be the greatest philosopher in the world, so completely do you have at hand and at your disposal every passage of this author. But it is my belief that the true book of the philosopher is the book of nature, which is always open before our eyes. But since it is written in characters different from those of our alphabet, it cannot be read by everyone. The characters of such a book are triangles, squares, circles, spheres, cones, pyramids and other mathematical figures entirely appropriate for such reading.[17]

THE SECULARIZATION OF SCIENCE

"The trial of Galileo," said Renan, "marks a decisive moment for the human spirit. At that moment scholasticism, devoid of sense, made up of an impossible mixture of the Bible and of Aristotle, both badly understood, found itself face to face with a veritable science which was capable of proving the truth of its claims." [18] The West, at last, was ready to throw off the double yoke of the Church and of Aristotle.

The eventual outcome of the seventeenth-century wave of religious persecution and intolerance was quite different from that which had swept over Islam five centuries earlier. The fanaticism of the Islamic rigorists thwarted the efforts of the Abbasids of the East and the Ommiads of Spain to create a rational and scientific culture. From the 12th century to today, the triumph of the Koran was assured. In Europe, on the contrary, the Faustian spirit born in the Renaissance gained in strength. The public rejected ecclesiastical condemnation of Galileo's *Dialogue*. Priests, monks and prelates competed with one another for copies on the "black market." [19] The Western mind had been aroused and had resumed the task of building science on the solid foundations of observation and mathematics.

At the beginning of the seventeenth century, there was not a single chair of mathematics in a European university. The one Galileo occupied for three years at Pisa carried a stipend of 60 écus at a time when professors of philosophy and of law received 1,000 écus. After Galileo, chairs of mathematics multiplied rapidly.

On the evening of January 8, 1642, three days before the death of Galileo, Isaac Newton was born. His synthesis of the findings of Kepler and Galileo was to establish, beyond possibility of doubt, the truth of the modern dynamics and astronomy for which Galileo had fought.

IX

THE NEW IMAGE OF
THE WORLD AND THE
IDEA OF PROGRESS

THE CLOSED WORLD OF ARISTOTLE

For generations, humanity lived in a closed and intellectually comfortable world, the structure of which had been worked out by Greek geometry. The *De coela* (On the Heavens) of Aristotle seemed to have given the definitive picture of the universe, consisting of two distinct regions. The celestial world, composed of an incorruptible essence, extended from the orbit of the moon to the sphere of the stars. The sublunary world, composed of an unstable mixture of four elements—earth, air, fire, and water—was located within the convexity of the orbit of the moon. This was the region of becoming, of change, of generation and of corruption, with the earth as its center. The human soul was a spark torn from the celestial fires, fallen into the tomb of the body as a consequence of some personal cosmic sin, and destined to return eventually to its starry home, there to live eternally.

Such was the vision of the world which enchanted the man of antiquity. Raising his eyes heavenward, each man could contemplate the radiant faces of the stars, and see there the guardian divinities who observed everything happening on earth, whose gaze was so all-encompassing that no secret crime could go unpunished. Contemplation of the cosmos aroused in the Greeks, and their Roman disciples, no sentiment of fear, no feeling of abandonment; rather, feelings of comfort, admiration and gratitude. The universe appeared to exist to serve man in this world, and to provide him with a glorious abode in the next. He saw himself as the king of creation, located in the center of a world created for his use and subordinated to his ends.

This image of the world was not entirely abandoned with the triumph of Christianity. True, the world ceased to be regarded as eternal; it had a beginning, and it would have an end. In place of the astral polytheism of the Greeks and early Romans there was substituted a Judeo-Christian monotheism based on the idea of a creator God who transcended the world. The Greek belief in the celestial immortality of souls was combined, not entirely successfully, with the Semitic belief in the resurrection of the body on the Day of Judgment. Though the stars ceased to be seen as gods, they were nonetheless thought to be guided in their paths by angels. But the structure of the world remained the same; it simply became more complex to take account of the teaching of the Scriptures. To the sky of the fixed stars was added another, a crystalline sky, capped by the Empyrean—the resting place of the Trinity, the Virgin and the Saints.

At the center of the universe, above a horrifying and shadowy hell from which seductive devils continually issued, stood the stationary earth, where man, fallen but redeemed, was free to choose between good and evil. He was perpetually prey to the entrapments of Satan, but he was also sustained by the grace of God, the protection of the Virgin and the intercession of the Saints. Such was the image of the world which inspired the Middle Ages and which found eloquent expression in Dante's *Divine Comedy*. It was more dramatic than that of the ancients, but it was still fitted to the measure of man, who remained the center of interest.

THE OPEN WORLD OF GALILEO

This mental picture of the cosmos was shattered by the discoveries of Kepler, Galileo and Newton. The closed and structured world of the ancients and Scholastics was replaced by an infinite universe, the center of which is everywhere and the circumference nowhere. The earth was no longer a privileged star; it was simply one small planet circulating around the sun, carried along in its dizzy course in the midst of a galaxy which Herschel would reveal to be itself lost in an infinity of other galaxies. Man ceased to be the king of creation, and the idea would necessarily arise that there might be a number of other worlds.

Fallen from his preeminence, man became aware that he was alone in an alien world. The indifference of nature was a theme to be exploited by Diderot and the Romantics. But man also began to see that, with the aid of science, he could better his condition. The pessimism engendered by the collapse of the image of the world of the ancients was replaced by the optimistic notion of perpetual improvement.

THE IDEA OF PROGRESS

With the scientific revolution appeared an idea destined to differentiate Western civilization from Hindu, Chinese, African and pre-Columbian civilizations—the conception of progress.

In Egypt, Sumeria and Babylon, science had been the monopoly of priests and scribes, who guarded it as a revelation from an arcane past. The more ancient a doctrine, the more it was revered. In Greco-Roman antiquity, most philosophical sects believed in the endless repetition of events, turning inexorably in the same circle, governed by the revolution of the stars. Lucretius, the Roman poet, had painted a magnificent picture of human development with his description of man's triple drives of need, experience, and reason; but this development was not "progress," in the sense of an endless, unilinear growth. On the contrary, when he considered the degeneracy of the world in which he lived, Lucretius could only look back with regret to an earlier, happier era, when an exuberant nature provided for the needs of a rustic and vigorous race.[1] Horace, long before Rousseau, deplored the corruption which civilization brought in its wake. "Our fathers were worse than our forefathers. We have degenerated from our fathers; our sons will bring us sorrow."[2] Civil and religious institutions, customs, and manners tended to insulate social organisms, to block change and to neutralize external disturbances. The castes, the closed and hereditary professions found in India and Egypt at certain times, the social structure of the Late Empire, and the rules and regulations of the corporations of the Middle Ages, all provided striking examples of this tendency. Even during the nineteenth century, economists would study with special care the mechanisms of equilibrium. We shall have to wait until 1940 before Colin Clark sheds light upon the problems of growth.

In the course of the seventeenth and eighteenth centuries, and in the West only, man ceased to turn backward, to regret a lost paradise, a Golden Age, or a sunken Atlantis. For the first time, he looked to the future with confidence and hope, and saw antiquity as it really was—the infancy of the world. Blaise Pascal, in the preface to his *Traité du Vide,* noted that knowledge was cumulative, and that the antiquity so revered in the men of the distant past was actually to be found in contemporary man. The greatest respect and gratitude which could be shown the ancients, he argued, would be to go beyond them rather than to rest on their authority: "It is in this way that we acknowledge the debt we owe them. Because, having been raised to the particular level to which they have carried us, the least effort enables us to mount still higher. . . . Yet . . . men count it a crime to contradict them, or to add anything to them, as if they had left no truths to be discovered. Is that not unworthy of human reason?" [3]

TURGOT, BUFFON AND CONDORCET

The perfectibility of man and the limitless progress of the human condition became controlling convictions of the eighteenth century. On the 11th of December, 1750, before the gentlemen of the Sorbonne, in the costume of the tonsured abbot—for he was destined for the Church—Anne Robert Jacques Turgot (1727–81), Baron de l'Aulne, delivered a discourse on *The Progress of the Human Spirit.* "The masses of mankind," the young baron told his august audience, "by alternating calm and agitation, marches always, though with slow steps, toward ever greater perfection." [4]

Buffon, the great French naturalist (1707–88), in the seventh and last of his *The Epochs of Nature,* sketched an immense fresco of the development of a world in which man had finally, though as yet imperfectly, come to realize his destiny. The powers conferred upon him by his intelligence would enable him to extract from nature new riches "without diminishing the treasures of her inexhaustible fecundity. And what could he not do to improve himself? . . . Who knows the limits of man's ability to perfect his own nature, physical or moral?" [5]

During the French Reign of Terror, the Marquis de Condorcet (1743–94), denounced and under arrest by the Convention, and living under the daily threat of the guillotine, devoted the last nine months of his life to writing the *Outline of the Progress of the Human Spirit,* a magnificent expression of faith in the future, thrown as an act of defiance at the heads of his persecutors. He wrote:

If man can predict with almost complete assurance the phenomena of which he understands the laws; if, even when they are unknown, he can, after the experience of the past, foresee with high probability the events of the future; why should anyone regard as a visionary enterprise the effort to trace with reasonable accuracy the tableau of the future destiny of the human species, according to the record of the past? Such is the purpose of the work which I have undertaken, . . . to show, by reason and by facts . . . that the perfectibility of man is really without limit, that the progress of this perfectibility, henceforth independent of all power which would stop it, has no other limit than the duration of the globe where nature has cast us.[6]

A new word, "happiness," had made its appearance in Europe, wrote Saint-Just, the French revolutionist, destined shortly, like Condorcet, to die under the guillotine (1794). Life was no longer conceived as a vale of tears where man's only purposes were sacrament and service. Man was born for happiness and not for the expiation of sin. In his *Essay on Man,* Pope proclaimed the Gospel of the new Beatitudes: "O Happiness! Our Being's End and Aim!" [7]

For once, Rousseau, Montesquieu and Voltaire were in agreement. "Happiness is the supreme end of all sensible beings," Emile's faithful mentor told him. "Happiness is the only object and purpose of all sensible human beings," affirmed Voltaire. Montesquieu was the author of an *Essay on Happiness.* Saint-Jean de Crèvecoeur, in *Letters from an American Farmer* (1782), reported that even in the savage solitude of the new world a laborer could find happiness. And in the Declaration of Independence of the United States, Jefferson put among the list of inalienable rights "the pursuit of happiness."

THE PHILOSOPHY OF HISTORY

In the eighteenth century, Western man became aware of his autonomy. In opposition to the astrological fatalism of the

Babylonians, from which a large number of the sects of antiquity had borrowed the idea of an eternal return, Christianity had offered a "celestial politics." In the Christian view, empires were raised up or cast down by the hand of God, according to a providential plan about which man could do nothing. In his *Discourse on Universal History*, Bishop Bossuet (1627–1704) had attributed the course of history to the desire of the Creator to ensure the triumph of Christianity. During the next century the perspective changed completely: humanity shaped its own destiny. The Neopolitan jurist and philosopher, Giambattista Vico (1668–1774), would emphasize this idea in his *Scienza Nuova,* in which he argued that humanity was created by humanity and recorded by humanity, since a being who creates himself at the same time knows himself: ". . . this world of ours was made by men. It is therefore possible, since it is useful and necessary, to discover its principles in the modification of our own spirit." [8]

Vico developed what would become Auguste Comte's (1798–1857) law of the three stages, and inspired, in an entirely different but illuminating manner, Voltaire's *Essay on Morals,* Turgot's *Discourse,* and Condorcet's *Outline.* Voltaire was the first to use the term "philosophy of history." Only through philosophy was the meaning of history to be discovered. Numerous interpretations would be proposed in the nineteenth and twentieth centuries, notably those by Hegel, Comte, Alexis de Tocqueville, Karl Marx, Friedrich Nietzsche, Herbert Spencer, Max Weber, Oswald Spengler, and Arnold Toynbee. For the most part they would conclude with Giambattista Vico that man was the conscious and responsible artisan of his own destiny, that he was not a passive instrument, that there was no cosmic or supernatural force which he could invoke as an excuse or alibi.

In 1831, in his *Introduction to Universal History,* Jules Michelet gave the philosophy of history an interpretation which summed up the new spirit of Western civilization.

"With the beginning of the world began a war which will not finish until the world is finished: this is the war of man against nature, of the spirit against matter, of liberty against fatalism. History is nothing else but the recital of this interminable struggle." [9]

THE PROTESTANT ETHIC
AND THE APPEARANCE OF
THE CAPITALIST MENTALITY

The rehabilitation of manual labor in the course of the Middle Ages would not have sufficed in and of itself to encourage the accumulation of capital and produce the Western economic system. A new entrepreneurial mentality, closely connected with the rise of commerce and the Protestant Reformation, was to mark this turning point in modern history.

THE ECONOMY OF THE ANCIENT WORLD

To understand the significance of this mentality, it is necessary to recall conditions in the Greco-Roman world from which our civilization sprang.

A characteristic of ancient civilizations was the lowly place assigned to economic activities and the sharp limitations placed upon their exercise. Public attitudes toward labor, free or slave, varied from city to city in ancient Greece as well as in Rome and in the provinces, depending upon the social strata from which those in power at any particular time came. Athens had known an economic imperialism, just as republican Rome had experienced a plutocracy of bankers. The judgment of the intellectual elite, however, was much the same everywhere. In Xenophon, Plato, Aristotle or Cicero, one finds the same doctrine affirmed: the mechanical and industrial arts deform the body and debase the soul. They are the enemies of liberal culture and the development of generous sentiments, fit only for slaves predisposed by nature to such work. It was incumbent upon the freeman to undertake public duties and to defend the state. In fact, in all Greek cities where slavery prevailed, the citizen was a sort of *rentier,* freed of the need to look after himself and from worry about the means of his existence. These were tasks for slaves.

Plato and Aristotle both condemned the manifestations of capitalism in their time: commerce, foreign trade, credit, speculation and lending money at interest. They believed that economic activities, by their very nature, had to expand indefinitely, creating an excessive desire for wealth, arousing the greed of the poor and the cupidity of the rich, and provoking the class struggles which bring about the fall of the political order. The proper political order was a hierarchy governed by a small number of wise men who enforced justice and saw to it that only such economic activities were permitted as were required for the needs of a limited population.

The political system of Greece seldom exceeded the reach of a municipal organization. With Rome, although history opened upon a larger perspective, the political conceptions remained much the same. The social order rested upon the distinction between the humble (*humiliores*) and the noble (*honestiores*); the great masses of the people made up a vague collectivity called *turba* or *vulga,* terms of contempt which corresponded to Voltaire's *la canaille*—the rabble. The citizen passed his time at the forum and in the camps of the Praetorium. Trade was regarded as dishonorable: "The gain of every artisan is vile and nothing honorable can come out of a shop," wrote Cicero in *De officiis.*[1] The banker was held in contempt, and Cicero reserved true immortality for the great captains and magistrates of the past who had saved, succored and enlarged the country.

THE MORAL ECONOMY OF THE MIDDLE AGES

In some respects the society of the Middle Ages seemed to realize Plato's dream as set forth in *The Republic:* a stratified and aristocratic organization resting on three distinct classes: the serfs and craftsmen who assured the subsistence of the communities; a nobility who assured its defense; and a clergy who conducted men to supernatural objectives.

Manual work was regarded as a necessity, ordained by nature and a consequence of original sin. Anyone under no necessity to work should refrain in order to give himself more fully to study and prayer. Voluntary poverty and the begging which necessarily resulted from it were superior to wealth and work, because poverty, as exalted by the mendicant orders, was a beatitude, and the poor were in "the image of Christ."

Inevitably, this view of life disparaged commerce, the motive of which was personal enrichment. The merchant was despised by the Church. "The merchant can only with great difficulty please God," declared an addition to a decree by Gratian, a monument of canon law in the twelfth century. "It is difficult not to sin when one makes a profession of buying and selling," proclaimed a decretal attributed variously to Leo the Great or to Gregory the Great. "Commerce, considered in itself, has a certain shameful characteristic," said Thomas Aquinas, "and rightly so, because of itself, it yields to the greed for gain (*lucrum*), and gain knows no limit." [2] In brief, because of the purpose behind it, commerce was regarded as one of the seven capital sins—avarice or cupidity.

Commerce was also despised because it led to usury, or the lending of money at interest. The scriptural texts were strict. Deuteronomy stipulated: "Thou shalt not lend money upon usury to thy brother; usury of money, usury of victuals, usury of any thing that is lent upon usury." [3] Jesus said: "And if ye lend to them of whom ye hope to receive, what thanks have ye? for sinners also lend to sinners, to receive as much again. But love ye your enemies, and do good, and lend hoping for nothing again; and your reward shall be great." [4] Aristotle was not less strict: "Money is barren." To these strictures, theologians and economists added what seemed a decisive argument: the taking of interest was equivalent to the selling of time, and time belonged to no man, because it belonged to God.

Production was submitted to minute regulations under corporate and canon law. Medieval commerce occurred in a *moralized economy* which undertook to establish just wages and prices, and to guarantee the quality of merchandise. Advertising was forbidden on the belief that it involved taking another man's clientele. To try to produce goods of a higher quality than one's colleagues was considered disloyal. In the corporation, everything was regulated: the length of apprenticeship, the number of co-workers, the level of salaries, the hours of work and the techniques of production. Not the most rapid and efficient procedure, but the slowest and the most painstaking, was preferred. All innovation was suspect and could be introduced only after preliminary agreement with the elders of the corporation and the judges of the city.

In this hierarchical society, everyone was expected to behave according to his social condition. The peasant and artisan were to be paid their due. The nobleman was to live with dignity and honor; his money should be spent, not hoarded or invested. He was the bearer of the traditions of chivalry; he was expected to despise money and to spend it lavishly on churches, castles, pious endowments, tournaments, hunts and fairs. The Church condemned neither public nor private magnificence. To cultivate the arts and make them serve religion in accordance with the norms of the councils was to glorify the Creator; it was deemed pious to surround the divine services with pomp and ostentation. The Church practiced triumphalism.

CALVINISM: A TURNING POINT

The Church of the Middle Ages had little understanding of commercial and economic matters. It regarded the work of the husbandman on the land and the artisan in the town as the source of wealth; trade only passed from hand to hand what had already been produced. But after the twelfth century, with the development of commerce on a larger scale, theologians and canon lawyers had to make concessions. They were forced to recognize that the merchant incurred risks which could result in real losses, that money tied up in a loan involved the sacrifice of a possible and legitimate gain elsewhere, that the trader who voyaged far afield at great risk and peril in search of provisions and goods not locally available performed a useful service. Over the years the Church came to accept interest on public loans, contracts, and bills of exchange as useful and legitimate. The inflations of the thirteenth century made abundantly clear the risks run by all lenders. "If uncertainty and risk do not fully atone for the spirit of gain, that is, if they do not excuse usury, . . . at least they produce results that are not unjust," was a conclusion of the subtle Gilbert de Messine.[5] Acceptance of the legitimacy of interest was made the easier as the Church began to recruit its priests from the merchant classes. The mendicant orders, paradoxically, provided the most spirited defenses of the merchants. The Papacy was similarly influenced; Innocent IV came from a wealthy Genoa merchant family; Leo X and Clement VII were Medicis.

With the discovery of the New World, trading took on added importance. Comforts multiplied. Urban life was transformed, particularly in the great nation-states which were taking shape. The stage was set for the moral and economic revolution known as the Reformation.

Lutheranism in its beginnings gave little hint of what was coming. Martin Luther (1483–1546) was the son of a peasant and was raised according to the patriarchal ideals of the prophets of Israel. His political and social views were medieval and feudal. Work was a punishment (*remedium peccati*); to take interest on loans was sinful; to want more wealth than was required to live in one's accustomed manner was evidence that one was not in a state of grace. Luther denounced the great trading and banking companies of his day, such as the Lombards, who enjoyed what he regarded as the sinful protection of godless parliaments and kings.

Nevertheless, Luther's doctrines of vocations and justification by faith foreshadowed profound changes. Since salvation was the free gift of God's grace and not the result of sacraments, prayers and asceticism, why live a sterile and lonely life? All conditions of life, all callings and vocations, were equal in the eyes of the Lord. The life of the lay brother was no less worthy than that of the priest; indeed, in some respects it was superior. The work of the craftsman was more useful than the idleness of the monk who selfishly washed his hands of worldly responsibility. To find out whether one belonged to the saved, one pursued his calling well and diligently. The surest way to show one's love for God was to serve one's neighbor.

It was Calvinism, however, which developed the full consequences of this outlook. John Calvin (1509–64), the son of a middle-class family, was a lawyer as well as a theologian, who by chance became the head of a state. Instead of distinguishing the temporal from the spiritual—as the Catholic Church did—and the political from the religious—as the Lutherans did—Calvin returned to the theocratic ideal of the Bible and insisted on putting all human actions on an equal

Christian footing. Eliminated for the first time since antiquity was the tragic divorce between sacred life and secular life, between spiritual and temporal interests, between the City of God and the city of man. This was done not by subordinating one to the other, but by recognizing their mutual interpenetration. The daily life of ordinary citizens was, in Calvin's view, superior to the useless existence of the monks. Work was not a consequence of natural law or original sin; nor was it an act of asceticism designed to protect one against evil temptations. Calvin elevated it to the dignity of a divine service.

The impact of the Reformation was to shift men's minds from the quest for mere personal and individual salvation to a wider concern. The glory of God was best served by acts which promoted the general good and improved the human condition. Callings, even the most mundane, were seen as divine instruments through which men realized God's plan. Work was transformed from a punishment into a religious vocation.

From all this it followed that not only sloth, idleness and mendacity were damnable, but also luxury, prodigality, ostentation, the pomp of the Catholic Church and the extravagance of royal courts. Calvin did not rise above the mentality of the small bourgeois of the Geneva of his time, but, wittingly or unwittingly, his praise of work and of parsimony (which the Scholastics had denounced as a leprosy of the soul) inevitably led to an accumulation of capital and thus stimulated the mammonism he condemned.

The economy of the Middle Ages had produced considerable wealth in the form of cathedrals, castles, town halls, statuary, tapestries, etc. (what economists of today would call consumer goods). There was no corresponding creation of productive capital, as the term is now understood. As this form of accumulation gained importance, however, a new spirit appeared. Calvin, head of an industrial and trading city, with his acute appreciation of the needs of business, recognized the importance of money and credit as means of facilitating exchange, and the legitimacy of a reward for a money loan. He distinguished sharply, however, between interest and usury, between a reasonable and an exorbitant return on money.

Assuming the return was reasonable, it was a matter of indifference whether a man's profit came from trading in money or in goods, since money represented commodities. Thus Calvinism, and in particular the Puritan sects which sprang from it, spread the mantle of righteousness over most economic activities. Inevitably this glorification of work and condemnation of pleasure provided the indispensable conditions for the appearance of modern capitalism.

THE PROTESTANT ETHIC AND MODERN CAPITALISM

But not immediately. Calvin was a deeply religious man who defended the money maker because of the help he could render the poor. The rich were rich only that they might fulfill God's will, which was that they give of their abundance to succor the poor, who represent the presence of Christ among men. Calvin was more concerned with how men used their wealth than with how they accumulated it. But over time attention shifted increasingly to the importance of accumulating wealth. This was particularly true of the Puritans, the Pietists and the Methodists.

The Presbyterian Richard Baxter (1615–91) condemned wealth as the source of all evils, yet made it clear that this was because it led to idleness. The sin of the wealthy was that they gave thought only to the enjoyment of their wealth. The law of work, however, was unconditional; it applied to rich and poor alike. Life was action, and only action could glorify God; repose and idle pleasure were the deadly sins. "It is permissible to work to become rich, so long as it be not for the joys of the flesh and sin, but for the accomplishment of God's will." [6] The rich man was God's trustee and should put to good use the wealth the Lord had entrusted to him. This was the whole meaning of the parable of the bad servant who failed to increase the wealth of his master. If God offered one of his children a chance for gain, He had something in mind, and not to seize the chance was to do injury to His providence. "It is permissible to strive to make the largest possible profit. It is your duty to use and to develop to the full your faculties and your talents." [7] John Wesley, the founder of Methodism, was equally emphatic: "Religion necessarily engenders love of work and sobriety, and these two virtues cannot but produce wealth. . . . We should encourage the Christian to make and to save all he can and in consequence to enrich himself." [8]

The Puritans also attached great importance to sobriety of dress and bearing, as well as to simplicity of food and speech. As the Protestant ethic replaced the medieval Catholic ethic, a capitalistic mentality emerged. It encouraged the poor to accept the discipline of work, and the rich to accumulate capital through frugal living and the reinvestment of gains. The resulting standardization of goods and services paved the way for the miracle of mass production. The economic virtues, industry and frugality, replaced the theological virtues.

The Calvinistic ethic ushered in the spirit and practice of capitalism so completely that success in business was all too frequently taken as evidence of divine election. Despite its view that man's actions do not alter God's choices, Calvinism marked a return to the ancient Semitic conception of rewards in this world for the righteous. We see its early expression in the Book of Job where the man of property who stood fast in adversity lived to see his flocks doubled and was blessed with descendants. On every page of Proverbs, the book of wisdom for the average Israelite, is found assurance that wealth is a blessing from God. The glorification of work of necessity brought in its train a respect for wealth.

THE SECULARIZATION OF THE PROTESTANT ETHIC

The Protestant ethic also explains the rapid advance of the Anglo-Saxon countries over the Catholic countries and even the Lutheran countries. It engendered a new mentality, utterly unknown to the man of the Middle Ages, obsessed as he was with the idea of salvation, and unknown still to most of the peoples of the earth—the pursuit of gain with a view to personal enrichment. The great masses in the underdeveloped countries see no need for work beyond that needed to assure their immediate subsistence. As in the England of Shakespeare, the average man in these countries has as his goal, not the improvement, but the maintenance of his customary way of life. For modern capitalism to grow, the economic virtues preached by the Protestant sects have to penetrate into every stratum of society and turn men's minds to the problems of this world.

For the Anglo-Saxon countries, this profound change was largely accomplished during the eighteenth century, concomitant with the development of the Industrial Revolution. No one is more representative of this new mentality than a man who fascinated two continents and whose wisdom was regarded as the Bible of a new era—Benjamin Franklin.

Born under the somber skies of Puritanism, Franklin (1706–90) found the spiritual climate of Boston so oppressive that at the age of seventeen he departed for Philadelphia, William Penn's city of brotherly love and freedom of thought. But deep within his rebellious soul he carried his ancestors' Calvinistic convictions about the virtues of prudence, sobriety, work and frugality. Long before Rockefeller or Ford, he wrote the book which summed up the Protestant ethic. Over a period of twenty-five years, he poured it forth in the pages of his *Poor Richard's Almanack* in the form of homely advice on the art of making money. He summed it all up in a passage in one issue of the *Almanack* which was translated into many languages and widely circulated under the title of *The Way To Wealth.*

All of Franklin's wisdom is expressed in the maxim, "Time is Money." The value of time and the importance of frugality were concisely expressed in such famous aphorisms as the following: "Dost thou love life? Then do not squander Time, for that's the stuff Life is made of." "The sleeping Fox catches no Poultry." "Lost time is never found again." "Early to Bed and early to rise, makes a Man healthy, wealthy and wise." "If you would be wealthy, think of Saving as well as Getting." [9]

From the back of his printing shop he preached the gospel of capitalism, based on work, saving, accumulation, efficiency and a sense of social service. A new philosophy, utilitarianism, replaced the existing systems of metaphysics. Adam Smith based his political philosophy on it, showing how the invisible hand of competition forced private interests to serve the public interest. Henceforth, the movement which had been given its forward thrust by the ethics of Calvin would emancipate itself from the limits of Protestant theology. A relentless internal necessity would force the capitalist system to proceed on a course of its own, freed from the religious beliefs which had supported it in its beginnings.

XI

THE ECONOMIC REVOLUTION

An economic revolution followed in the wake of the new Protestant ethic. During the eighteenth century the physiocrats in France and Adam Smith in England discovered the mechanisms of the market economy, a discovery which would transform accepted ideas about the creation and distribution of wealth, as will be noted in a later chapter, and the role of the state in the regulation of human relations.

ECONOMICS IN ANTIQUITY AND THE MIDDLE AGES

In Greco-Roman times, profit-seeking was considered beneath the dignity of the citizen. His task was to organize, administer and defend the city, not to provide for its material wants. Such economic tasks were left to the lower classes—to foreigners, freedmen and slaves. It was demeaning to the citizen to pay too much attention to these mundane matters. Consequently, except in the management of rural estates, no one thought to analyze the mechanisms underlying production and exchange.

Throughout the Middle Ages, life on earth was characteristically viewed as a preparation for a life hereafter. Theologians and canonists, following the traditions of the fathers of the Church, said the desire for wealth derived from sin; in the words of the Gospel, "It is easier for a camel to go through the eye of a needle, than for a rich man to enter into the kingdom of God." [1] The purpose of life is the pursuit of the supreme good, which by definition is something of which a man can never have enough. The pursuit of wealth quickly leads to satiety. Only through the contemplation of God, the infinite Being, can man aspire to infinite bliss.

The idea of an economy based on the free play of supply and demand could not be envisioned by men of the Middle Ages for several obvious reasons. During the High Middle Ages, rural property was the economic unit around which were assembled serfs, peasants and craftsmen, all under the protection of the lord of the manor. There were no free exchanges among the members of this community. The lord of the manor provided his serfs with certain services—protection in case of danger, the use of his oven and mill—and in return the serfs had to turn over a part of their crops. The manor was self-sufficient. Land was not something to be bought and sold; in the hands of the Church it was inalienable, and it never occurred to the nobility to dispose of their holdings. Land would not become a vendible good until it had been freed from religious and feudal restrictions.

With the rise of cities and the growth of urban population there developed a division of labor. The inhabitants of the countryside concentrated increasingly on the production of agricultural commodities, while the city dwellers specialized in the transformation of these commodities and in the fabrication of goods. Exchanges developed between town and country, but these were subject to the decrees of the corporations and canonical rules about just prices and rates of interest. True, the kings were greedy for treasure and made war in order to amass wealth, and the ambition of the nobles was to expand their estates; but the majority of the people—serfs, artisans, and masters of the guilds—sought only to live as their fathers before them had lived, and to pass on the same kind of life to the succeeding generation.

The great geographical discoveries of the fifteenth century

and the displacement of feudal principalities by nation-states shattered this ancient pattern. Local markets yielded to national markets and then to international exchanges. The influx of gold and silver from the mines of the New World caused inflation, gave rise to controversies over monetary policy, and to the belief that the accumulation of precious metals increased the power of the state. This belief marks the beginning of the Age of Mercantilism,[2] a transitional period falling between the Middle Ages, with its emphasis on status, and the Age of Modern Capitalism, with its emphasis on contract.

MERCANTILISM AND ECONOMIC WARFARE

While all European countries at this time sought to accumulate treasure, their methods varied. Spain required all ships leaving its ports to bring back precious metals equal in value to their outgoing cargoes, and all ships entering its ports to take out goods equal only to a part of what they brought in. In France, the government tried to increase the monetary stock by encouraging the export of luxuries. In England and Holland, the governments likewise counted on international trade to increase their stocks of precious metals.

Mercantilism rested on two fallacies. The first consisted in regarding metallic currency per se as wealth. From this it followed that the aim of policy was always to sell, never to buy. The second was the belief that there was only a given amount of wealth in the world; consequently, one nation could wax rich only at the expense of its neighbors. These fallacious beliefs led governments to encourage exports by subsidies and to discourage imports by high tariffs, and to use state interventions to encourage domestic enterprises. The aim of policy was to build up through a favorable balance of trade the "war chest" in gold and silver needed to assure victory in war, increase the national patrimony through annexation of conquered territories, and prevent civil wars deriving from "malevolent humours" in the kingdom. Louis XIV's great minister, Colbert, developed the system to such a point of logical perfection that in France "Colbertism" has become a synonym for mercantilism.

The inevitable outcome of Colbertism was economic warfare. It was directly responsible for the war against the Dutch and the War of the League of Augsburg. The Dutch, the English and the Germans followed the same policy as the French.

FREE TRADE AND PEACE

The great discovery of Turgot and the physiocrats in France and of Adam Smith and his liberal followers in England can be stated very briefly. Wealth is not limited. It can be increased almost indefinitely by specialization and exchange. Hence the aim of public policy should be to promote the greatest possible freedom of trade within and among nations. Mercantilism, by seeking to make trade a one-way affair, inevitably leads to autarchy, militarism and war. Free trade, on the other hand, leads to a balance of imports and exports, the interdependence of nations, and the substitution of contract for force.

THE FRENCH PHYSIOCRATS

While Smith and the physiocrats were not the first to see the potential benefits of free trade,[3] they were the first to provide a rigorous demonstration.

François Quesnay (1694–1774), physician to Madame de Pompadour, held that wealth comes from production and that as it passes from hand to hand it invigorates the body politic just as blood sustains the human body. In his *Tableau Economique*, Quesnay described the manner in which wealth is created in the realm of agriculture and is circulated through a thousand channels—among landowners, industrialists and traders. These latter merely transform and circulate wealth created by agriculture with the help of nature.

The physiocrats insisted that the creation and distribution of wealth obeyed natural laws which man could discover by the use of reason. The laws were thought to rest on a natural order willed by God for the happiness of man; local and state authorities should take care not to disturb this order. The physiocrats explained that in France internal barriers to trade and the fear of later scarcities were responsible for "imprisoning wheat." In some provinces wheat rotted in the granaries while people starved in other provinces where there had been crop failures. In 1774, Turgot ordered that grain should be allowed to circulate freely throughout the country, and Gournay gave to the world his famous formula: *"laissez faire, laissez passer."*

This formula became a weapon for beating down the internal and external trade walls separating peoples. It was justified by appeal to a natural and providential order which spontaneously adapts production to consumption, through the laws of supply and demand operating in competitive markets. The role of the sovereign was to see that the play of these forces was not distorted by coalitions of selfish interests. Mercier de la Rivière stated the underlying principle:

By a law of nature, the particular happiness of each nation is destined to increase the general happiness of other nations: to profit from this fortunate circumstance, they need do no more than avoid placing impediments on the liberty which tends to bring them together, to unite them, making them into a single society.[4]

ADAM SMITH AND THE MARKET ECONOMY

Adam Smith's *Wealth of Nations* (1776) laid the foundations of a new science of political economy. Smith sought to show, on the basis of observations, that the natural order of the physiocrats grew spontaneously out of psychological motives which govern men, motives willed by the Creator and purged of taint by the Protestant ethic.

The purpose and end of production is consumption; hence the wealth of a nation consists in the totality of the goods and services enjoyed by the people, not in the precious metals amassed in the royal treasury. Society is not divided into productive and sterile classes, as the physiocrats claimed—excepting always the idlers. The annual product of the nation is the result of collaboration among all classes on the basis of a division of labor, which increases the productivity of the workers and the wealth of the nation in direct proportion to the intensity with which it is practiced. A visit to a pin factory permitted Smith to illustrate this truth: A group of ten men, each specializing on one small part of the total task, could produce 48,000 pins a day, whereas if each man tried to make the entire pin, the group of ten would not be able to produce more than 200 pins a day.[5]

How does this division of labor operate? In a society that wants to grow in wealth, like the England of Smith's day, the goal of individual self-interest leads men to do the work society will pay for: "It is not from the benevolence of the butcher, the brewer, or the baker that we expect our dinner, but from their regard to their own interests. We address ourselves, not to their humanity but to their self-love, and never talk to them of our own necessities but of their advantages." [6]

Self-interest leads everyone to try to sell his services for as much as he can get, and to pay as little as possible for what he gets from others. But competition exercises a moderating influence. Let a trader put too high a price on his merchandise, or refuse to pay his workers the rate paid by his competitors, and what happens? In the first case, he loses his customers; in the second, his workers. If the state does not interfere, prices and wages will settle spontaneously at levels permitting traders to meet competition and satisfy their clientele. Such is the law of the market.

The law of the market is nothing more than the law of supply and demand operating on prices. It ensures that producers respond, in quantity and quality, to the needs of society. If consumers prefer gloves to shoes, the price of gloves rises from the pressure of demand, while the price of shoes descends. The glovemakers whose revenues have increased will enlarge their operations, while the shoemakers, seeing their profits falling, will reduce theirs. But as more gloves reach the market in response to the demand of consumers, the price will return to normal. The price mechanism will have reshaped production to meet the wishes of consumers, without any preestablished plan from a central authority—provided there is free competition.

The same thing will happen with respect to the income allotted to the various factors of production. If profits in one branch of production are particularly high, new enterprises will be attracted and prices will decline. If an industry offers higher wages than others, it will attract additional workers until their abundance will bring wages back to the level paid by other enterprises requiring workers of comparable skill.

In brief, whether it be in labor markets, or the capital markets, or in markets where goods and services are exchanged, the law of supply and demand will establish wages, profits and interest at equilibrium levels, permitting all offers to be accepted and all demands to be satisfied. But the price mechanism does more than account for this universal equilibrium; it also accounts for the dynamics of growth. The forces which motivate individuals to increase their incomes operate for whole societies. Men naturally want to improve their condition, and this leads them to save and to invest their savings productively. The result, as the Protestant preachers had clearly realized, is an accumulation of capital.

The rapid changes going on in Smith's time permitted businessmen to make fortunes from their investments. Richard Arkwright, a barber's apprentice, left an estate of 500,000 pounds sterling. Such accumulations of capital permitted the construction of new machines and a more elaborate division of labor, thus increasing the productivity of workers and the total wealth of the society.

As production increased, so did the need for manpower. The result was a rise in wages which increased production costs, reduced profits and the possibilities for reinvestment. The growth of the economy might have been halted had it not been for a new stimulant in the form of an increase in the working population. The infant mortality rate was shockingly high. "It is not uncommon in the Highlands of Scotland," Smith noted, "for a mother who has borne twenty children not to have two alive." [7] The increase in wages permitted families to raise their children with a more favorable rate of survival. As the number of workers increased, the competition among them checked the rise in wages, although leaving them at a higher level than before. In this fashion the processes of growth went forward irregularly, speeding up when population growth slowed, slowing down when the growth of population spurted.

Smith approved of the increase in the real income of the workers, denying that it would foster laziness. On the contrary, he argued, the rise in wages led employers to provide their workers with better tools and improved working conditions, and at the same time improved the performance of the workers themselves.

A plentiful subsistence increases the bodily strength of the labourer, and the comfortable hope of bettering his condition, and of ending his days perhaps in ease and plenty, animates him to exert that strength to the utmost. Where wages are high, accordingly, we shall always find the workman more active, diligent and expeditious than where they are low: in England, for example, more than in Scotland; in the neighbourhood of great towns more than in remote country places.[8]

How contrary Smith's optimistic views on wages were to those of the ancients ("For a society to be prosperous, there must be slaves"), or of his contemporaries ("To make a society happy, it is necessary that great numbers should be wretched as well as poor").[9] The truth, Smith declared, is quite the opposite. Wages as high as the law of the market will support were advantageous for society. How could it be otherwise, he asked. "Servants, laborers, and workmen of different kinds make up the far greater part of every great political society. But what improves the circumstances of the greater part can never be regarded as an inconveniency to the whole. No society can surely be flourishing and happy, of which the far greater part of the members are poor and miserable." [10] So long as capital accumulation continued, a society could slowly but steadily improve the well-being of the masses, lifting them further and further above the level of abject poverty and misery.

What is true for one nation is true for all. Just as the true interests of the individual are in harmony with the general interest, so true national interests are in harmony with the international interest. States need only refrain from intervening in ways that prevent the spontaneous equilibrium favored by supply and demand. If the price mechanism is allowed to operate, the effort to produce at the lowest possible cost will bring about an ever-increasing division of labor among the nations. As they become more unified in their interests, the nations will find this harmony a guarantee of prosperity.

Adam Smith, disciple of Francis Hutcheson and friend of David Hume, invoked self-interest and the search for profit as the driving force of human activity. This sounds callous, but as Jeremy Bentham and John Stuart Mill would in due time point out, properly conceived self-interest has done more to reduce human misery than the charity which the Church of the Middle Ages preached and practiced. In his *Theory of Moral Sentiments* (1759), Adam Smith asked: "What purposes have labor and violent agitations served? What benefits do we derive from greed and ambition, from the pursuit of wealth, power and status?" [11] Seventeen years later, in *The Wealth of Nations*, he gave his answer: This powerful struggle for wealth and glory finds its justification in the well-being of the common man.

Everyone, he pointed out, tries to put his capital to the most profitable use. In so doing, "he intends only his own gain, and he is in this, as in many other cases, led by an invisible hand to promote an end which was not part of his intention. . . . By pursuing his own interest he frequently promotes that of the society more effectually than when he really intends to promote it." [12]

During the Middle Ages the Church had borne almost all the costs of public assistance. Other than the monasteries, which provided shelter for the sick, every town had its principal hospital, its Hotel Dieu. The Church laid its compassionate hands on the brows of the disinherited; she had words of consolation for the desperate. Yet she could avert neither periodic famines nor great plagues, like the Black Death (1348–50). Charity redistributed wealth, but could not create it. The creation of wealth results from the fact that the values achieved by an efficient combination of the factors of production are greater than the values consumed in the production process. Marx called this increment "surplus value"; professional economists now call it "added value." The creation of wealth is founded on natural resources, but these become economically valuable only as they are exploited by the intelligence and labor of men. Man's knowledge of natural processes and their use in his labors makes him a second creator—a veritable Prometheus.

The ills which Christian charity could reduce but not suppress were overcome by a market economy driven by self-interest and disciplined by competition, using the powers conferred on man by science and industry. The famines and the plagues which still periodically sweep through the under-developed countries, through India and China, have disappeared from Europe and from its privileged offspring, North America.

Smith's book had an immediate success and its influence spread rapidly. It was translated into French, German, Italian, Spanish and Danish. Pitt the Younger, at the time only a student, declared himself a disciple of Smith forever, and when he became prime minister he signed the first liberal treaty of commerce with France in 1786. Jean Baptiste Say, after reading *The Wealth of Nations,* wrote: "When one reads this work one realizes that prior to Smith there was no such thing as political economy." [13]

XII

THE INDUSTRIAL REVOLUTION

An industrial revolution went hand in hand with the economic revolution. What has come to be known as the Industrial Revolution involved a double substitution: Machines, driven by natural power, replaced tools driven by human muscle, and a reliable source of energy, the expansive power of steam, replaced sources like wind and falling water, which depended upon the configuration of the ground, climate, and the inclemencies of the weather.

The revolution transformed the economy of the West from one based on water and wood into one based on coal and iron. The face of the world was changed. Mills scattered along flowing rivers gradually gave way to manufacturing centers close to mines or existing cities. Factory smokestacks replaced church spires.

THE FIRST PHASE

The steam engine was the agent of this transformation. It was the outcome of a series of theoretical investigations extending back over several centuries. The details need not concern us here; however, without the contributions of such men as Boyle, Savary and Newcomen, James Watt's breakthrough would have been impossible.

While Watt was at work repairing a machine for Newcomen, he invented new ways to set in motion a number of separate mechanisms. He stopped losses of heat by insulating the cylinder, by creating the condenser, the slide valve and the governor; and he resorted to the old crankshaft known to the ancients and used in the Middle Ages, to transform the backward and forward motion of the piston and the balance wheel into a circular movement which could activate a variety of mechanisms. Thanks to his association with Matthew Boulton, the first steam engine (in the modern sense) was created at their plant in Soho in 1775, a machine destined to release a veritable revolution.

In metallurgical factories this engine powered bellows, rollers and hammers. It provided the power to grind grain for the miller, malt for the brewer, and silex for the potter, and to extract sugar from the canes brought from the distant Antilles. It drove Hargreaves's spinning jenny (1765), Arkwright's water frame (1768), Samuel Crompton's mule jenny, John Kay's flying shuttle (1788), and finally the power looms of Cartwright (1784) and Jacquard (1801).

If one were to fix on an exact date for Europe's industrial take-off, 1785 would be the year, seventeen years after Watt secured his first patent and the date of its termination. Henceforth the wealth of nations would be expressed in terms of steam (horsepower) and in tons of iron. In the next forty years, the spread of the steam engine produced an explosive transformation in men's ways of thinking and in their ways of life greater than in the preceding two thousand years.

In 1769 Josiah Wedgwood, who invented ways to mechanize pottery-making, presented a vivid picture of what had occurred in a single generation in his county in Cheshire: "In the beginning of the period, most of the homes were veritable huts. Fields were badly cultivated and yielded little for man or beast. Roads were wretched. Communication with other parts of the country was almost nonexistent. A generation later, workers were earning twice as much as before; their homes were for the most part new and comfortable. Fields were well cultivated and roads were well maintained." [1]

Yet the use of the steam engine spread slowly, prior to the discovery of the secret of thermodynamics by Sadi Carnot, the perfection of the converter by Henry Bessemer (1856) and the introduction by the Martin brothers of their improved method of converting iron into steel. As late as 1851, England was producing only 60,000 tons of steel. By 1899 her production had risen to 3,637,000 tons, and the United States was producing 4,346,000 tons. In the 150 years following the 1785 "take-off," world production of coal increased a hundredfold, while that of steel and iron rose more than four hundredfold.

THE SECOND PHASE

Before the century had passed, a second revolution had started, ushered in by the discovery of oil. This new source of energy was first found in Ohio in 1859. It would shortly power turbines, thanks to Grammes's invention of the dynamo (1872), and with the invention of gasoline and diesel engines, it revolutionized transportation by land and water. Then came the discovery of electricity, which could be transmitted cheaply over long distances. It was used to power railroads and, after Bell's invention of the telephone, to send the human voice over vast distances with almost the speed of sound. In due time natural gas provided still another source of power; and then after World War II came the development of nuclear power.

Meantime, advances in chemistry opened up vast possibilities in fields as diverse as dyes, detergents, explosives, fertilizers, perfumes, medicines, synthetic foods, artificial textiles, plastics, silicones and alloys. All of these are the products of the new science of chemistry which Lavoisier and Berthollet had created out of the medieval practice of alchemy.

THE AGRICULTURAL REVOLUTION

Overlapping these two revolutions was still a third, in agriculture. It repealed, for the West at least, the Malthusian law of hunger, ended the famines which had plagued peoples, and permitted the Free World in time to help feed the Communists (whose agriculture has been their Achilles' heel) and the peoples of the "underdeveloped" nations.

This agricultural revolution goes back to the early eighteenth century, well before the beginnings of the Industrial Revolution. It started with improvements in methods of cultivation. The abandonment or reduction in fallowing created opportunities for raising plants suitable as fodder; crop rotation made possible the growing of industrial crops like beets, rapeseed and cotton, and encouraged intensive market gardening. These improved practices were vastly accelerated with the development of chemical fertilizers. Liming and dunging had been the only processes used to improve the soil, and the only known fertilizers had been animal droppings, Irish moss and seaweed. With the publication of Liebig's *Chemistry in Its Application to Agriculture and Physiology* (1840), the era of chemical fertilizers began. Henceforth, it was possible to feed any soil the three nourishing elements, phosphorus, nitrogen and potassium, in whatever proportions were needed for maximum production. Within a century, tenfold increases in yields per acre were obtained.

Mechanization produced a third transformation in agriculture. In 1833 came the McCormick reaper; in 1868 the combine; in the twentieth century, these and other labor-saving machines were motorized; the first tractor dates from 1905, and the thresher-harvester from 1916.

These three developments—improvements in methods of cultivation, discovery of chemical fertilizers, and substitution of motorized machines for hand tools—increased yields per acre, and reduced the manpower and the arduousness of the labor needed to feed a rapidly growing population.

THE CYBERNETICS REVOLUTION

World War II laid the foundations for a third Industrial Revolution.

The *first* revolution had substituted for the muscular power of man and beast the artificial power derived from the energy of the sun stored up in peat, coal, oil and, finally, the energy of the atom. These energies made possible the *second* revolution, which expressed itself in the construction of motors of various sorts, from the steam engine to the atomic pile. When properly harnessed, they gave rise to a great diversity of machine tools in the form of locomotives, automobiles, airplanes, tractors, excavators, etc.

To realize the way in which these machine tools reduced human labor, consider the following: a man working 2,500 hours in the course of a year releases approximately 100 kilowatts of energy, which is what a motor produces with 40 kilos of coal or 15 litres of oil. One mechanical slave is thus produced every time 40 kilos of coal are brought to the surface of a mine, or when 15 litres of oil are refined.

Prior to the nineteenth century, there were relatively few such mechanical slaves. By 1850, there may have been as many as 3 billion; by 1900, 20 billion; and by 1950, 70 billion. In a century enough power had been created to supply every living being with thirty mechanical slaves. Henceforth, the power of a country would be measured, not by the number of its inhabitants—otherwise China and India would be the most powerful countries on earth—but by horsepower, expressed in electrowatts available per inhabitant.

The first revolution turned upside down the social structures of the countries affected. It put an end to slavery; the wage earner in the factory replaced the serf on the land. It substituted for the guilds of craftsmen unions of workers and associations of business enterprises. Alongside the world of labor it developed various forms of capitalism—financial, commercial, industrial, private, collective and mixed. It transformed the earlier qualitative civilizations, based on an aristocracy of birth or on craft skills, into the industrial, democratic and quantitative civilizations of today.

Machine tools substituted muscles of steel for human brawn, but did not relieve man of the need to use his intellect. The worker on an assembly line, the foreman confronting a work schedule, and the engineer in charge, all had to be constantly on the alert, watching, controlling, correcting and repairing. The slightest slackening of attention could be catastrophic: a machine breaks down, a boiler explodes, a train takes a wrong turn. The modern worker uses his muscles much less and his brain much more than the slave of antiquity.

And now a *third* industrial revolution is in full course. It is creating "thinking" machines which relieve men of many mental tasks—machines which observe and store observations, compare them, select from among them, reason about them, and make decisions based on them. These new machines do not, of course, truly think, but they perform operations which, were they performed by human beings, would require what psychologists call observation, memory, reason and decision.[2]

The first cybernetic machines were self-regulating. They could, for example, keep constant the rotation of a motor which was subject to variable loads; as the speed of rotation increased, the electric current or steam pressure which operated the motor was automatically diminished, and vice versa. These self-regulating machines—the thermostats of refrigerators, automatic pilots on ships and airplanes—released the operator from an enormous amount of uninterrupted attention. But there have been two further advances. By supplying these mechanisms with sensory devices capable of memorizing, reasoning and making decisions, man has succeeded in relieving the human brain of many intellectual operations.

True, such robots are the products of man's ingenuity; he builds them; he gives them a structure capable of performing the operations he wants; they perform on his orders; they have to be supplied with instructions in a language they can use. Robots can answer questions; they cannot pose them, and the truly creative act consists of posing questions and projecting possible responses. The most perfect robots work by delegation; they accomplish only that which in man's intellectual activities is purely automatic and never that which constitutes genuine creativity.

Nonetheless, these robots have already revolutionized certain industries. They have made it possible for plants to operate entirely on an automatic basis. At Hartworth, England, for example, a fully automatic factory produces 500,000 electric light bulbs daily, beginning with the raw materials and ending with final packaging. At Sargrove-on-the-Thames, a plant empty of workers makes radio receivers at the rate of several million a month and at an incredibly low cost. At Betreville, France, one can see driverless tractors cultivating the soil; at Oak Ridge, Tennessee, the great sheds where fissionable materials are made are deserted. The chemical refineries at Aix-en-Provence are almost completely automatic. Coal is mined in the United States with equipment that bores, extracts, grinds and dumps the coal onto moving belts that take it to the surface, all without human effort. Mechanization has also produced what André Siegfried called the "secretarial revolution." It has penetrated into offices in the form of typewriters, dictaphones, tabulating machines, sorters, translating machines and copiers.

This freeing of men by automated machines foreshadows radical changes in our customs, in our individual and collective behavior and style of life, in the government of men, in the very structure of society, and even in our understanding of the world around us.

Before the end of this century, if we may believe the father of cybernetics, Norbert Wiener, much of American industry will be completely automatic, creating at once a greatly reduced need for blue-collar workers and an increased demand for engineers.[3] Most of the social and economic problems of present concern will be outmoded. With robots, strikes will be a thing of the past, as will be the present demands for social security, family allowances and similar welfare requirements. The forty-hour work week with overtime at penalty rates will become a historical curiosity. The robot will work twenty-four hours a day. Once machines are amortized, costs will fall precipitously.

Against these blessings must be balanced an enormous technological unemployment which will require a massive transfer of workers into what Colin Clark has called the third sector of the economy, the service sector, where needs are inexhaustible. With machines replacing workers, a new problem will emerge—the problem of leisure.

Cybernetics will do more than revolutionize production; it will penetrate into our family life, where the domestic servant is already disappearing, into our offices and public bureaus, from which the secretary-typist will eventually vanish. Methods of communication will be changed. The relations of men to their governments will be altered. Science will be transformed. It will be possible to solve complicated problems which have heretofore defied our greatest ingenuity. Physiology, neuro-psychology and the art of prothesis will be profoundly affected, thanks to the analogies we are discovering between the self-regulating cybernetic machines and biological regulations, and the transmission of orders through the nervous system. Science may tomorrow give to the blind new ways of reading, to the deaf new ways of hearing. The prospects are staggering.

This revolution is bound to produce a transvaluation of all our values. Civilizations based on manual skills and on an economy of scarcity exalted the passive virtues: patience, prudence and moderation, as extolled by the Stoics and the religions of salvation, which held forth the comforting hope of compensation in a world to come for injustices suffered on this earth. The first two revolutions produced civilizations which aimed at making man's present lot more comfortable. They substituted for the ancient passive virtues, and their supporting theologies, the active economic virtues preached by the great Protestant pastors: work, enterprise, efficiency and public service. Instead of poverty, the humble fiancée of St. Francis, the new theology substituted Benjamin Franklin's way to wealth.

Cybernetic civilizations, while preserving and multiplying the material well-being created by quantitative civilizations, may yet add the excellence of the earlier qualitative civilizations with their emphasis on beauty, internal perfection and spiritual contemplation. Ford and Gandhi, although irreducibly opposed to one another, may yet be reconciled in a new humanity—a breed of men who know how to combine a concern for social efficiency with an ideal of personal perfection.

XIII

THE POLITICAL REVOLUTION

The scientific revolution of the Renaissance, the ethical revolution of the Reformation, the discovery of the laws of the market, and the Industrial Revolution of the eighteenth century combined to produce a political revolution which completed the transformation of Western societies. As a larva breaks out of its chrysalis to form a more perfect insect, so these societies burst the framework of their *ancien régimes*. For the royal pleasure were substituted constitutions; for a hierarchical organization based upon privileges, equality before the law; for offices closed to the masses, free access to all positions; for the sovereignty of princes, sovereignty of the people; and for the omnipotence of the state, the rights of the human person.

This transformation was realized in a succession of revolutions stretching like links in a chain over the three-quarters of a century from 1770 to 1848. The changes, while seemingly abrupt, were in reality the outcome of a long historical process involving a continuing search for institutions capable of guaranteeing the individual against the omnipotent state.

CHRISTIANITY AND THE DISTINCTION BETWEEN THE TEMPORAL AND THE SPIRITUAL

All civilizations prior to the Christian era, with the exceptions of the Greek city-state and the Rome of the Republic,

[126]

rested on the deification of the state. Egyptian, Akkadian, Sumerian, Babylonian and Persian kings were all sons of gods or gods themselves. It was only in the democratic cities of Greece and in the Rome of the Republic that the state assumed a more abstract form. The citizen was protected by the law, but the law regulated customs and the dependence of the individual was still very great. Socrates rejected the proposal that he save his life by fleeing Athens, declaring that he was "a slave to the laws of the city." In republican Rome the public censors cast indiscreet looks into the most intimate details of family life. And with the passing of the Republic, the Roman emperors came increasingly to be worshiped by the provincials as gods (*dii*) and by the Romans as blessed (*divi*).

Christianity resisted this absolute subordination of the individual to the state. Even as the Jews had refused to worship Pharaoh, so Christians refused to burn incense before the statues of the deified Caesars. Above the earthly city was the heavenly city; above laws made by men were divine laws. Man was no longer the slave of the master of the moment; he was the slave of God. He had an inviolable conscience, a secret fastness where none might penetrate. He possessed an ideal of perfection higher than any *raison d'état,* any consideration of the needs of the state. The Christian martyr will always remain the prototype of the defender of the indefeasible rights of conscience.

Just as Christianity opposed the deification of the state, so too it destroyed the logical basis for aristocracy. The aristocratic constitutions of ancient societies rested on a belief in the diversity of origins of the human species. The right of the patrician families to give orders depended upon the belief that they were the descendants of gods or of heroes of the distant past.[1] Christianity, with its belief that the human race was descended from a single couple, rejected such ideas. It denied the conception of an aristocracy based on the law of nature. Aristocracies continued to exist, of course, but they were recognized as resting on past services or simply on the right of conquest.

True, the Church, as an institution with temporal interests, was usually found allied with the sovereigns, the nobles and the feudal lords; yet by denying the ideological foundations on which aristocratic governments rested, by providing an avenue for the claims of the poor and the weak, Christianity prepared the ground for and thus made possible the emergence of modern democracy. Its victory transformed Western societies and eventually promoted the development of democracy and its new *mystique* of equality.

Church organization was essentially hierarchical; yet its members were recruited from every walk of life. A simple shepherd could aspire to its highest office. And within the monasteries democratic procedures were observed. There were meetings of chapters, and questions of general interest were put to the vote at the plenary meetings of the church orders, to which each monastery sent its representative. Since the monks were without personal property and had no wives or children, equality within the monasteries was more than a simply theoretical notion. The medieval monasteries were veritable laboratories of democratic experimentation.

Christianity predisposed men to the spirit of democracy, but did not provide the direct inspiration for the political institutions which have protected the fundamental rights of the individual. Its aspiration was always toward theocracy, a society in which God was King and the pope His earthly vicar. The pope was pictured as holding two swords, the temporal and the spiritual, empowering him to crown kings and emperors and to depose them. Nonetheless, whenever the Church felt itself menaced by civil authorities it tried to enforce the distinction between the temporal and the spiritual.

Among the Protestant sects, Lutheranism ended up by accepting the subordination of the faithful to the established secular authorities in accordance with the celebrated formula, *cujus regio, ejus religio.* Calvin dreamed of a theocracy equally intolerant in the matter of opinions and of conduct. In this sense democracy, with its concern for the rights of man, cannot invoke in its support the doctrines of either the Catholic or the Protestant churches—at least not in the beginning.

MIXED GOVERNMENTS AND THE BALANCE OF POWER

In all organized societies a sharp distinction develops between the governed and the governors. The fact that men give up a part of their liberty and agree to obey one or several of their fellows is a necessary miracle of history; otherwise civilized living would be impossible. The alternative is anarchy. This abridgment of freedoms may be the temporary result of violence or of consent. In the first case it is only suffered, and changes as power relations change. In the second case it is mutually accepted; the wielders of power are regarded as holding it legitimately in accordance with the deliberate sentiment of the community.

Historically, the principle of legitimacy has rested on one of three foundations: the customs of the ancestors; divine right; the will of the people. No matter upon which of these foundations the claim to power rests, it tends to become abusive if it is unlimited. Custom is likely to condemn a society to immobility by imposing outworn rituals and meaningless constraints. Divine right leads to abuses under the cry, "It's God's will!" On the other hand, "It's the will of the people," can lead to popular dictatorship; in the name of the people from whom they claim to derive their powers, those in authority may impose their private wills. "The power of the people" is not always the same as "the liberty of the people."

As a society grows in wealth and no longer needs to devote

all its resources to defense, the governed tend to demand safeguards against the power of the governors. The question then arises: How can power be constitutionally limited?

Aristotle concluded from his study of some 180 constitutions that governments involving an admixture of the three forms were the best. The Roman Republic, according to both Cicero and Polybius, had realized this ideal. In the eighteenth century, Montesquieu echoed these judgments. Anticipating Lord Acton, he warned: "Any man with power is led to abuse it. He will push it until it meets a limit. . . . If power is not to be abused, it must be checked by another power." [2]

THE BEGINNING OF PARLIAMENTS:
THE HISTORIC RIGHTS OF THE ENGLISHMAN

Between the eleventh and the eighteenth centuries, England developed five institutions which served to safeguard individual liberties: (1) representation; (2) *habeas corpus;* (3) bicameralism; (4) constitutionalism, i.e., a political regime subject to rules superior to the government itself; and (5) parliamentarianism. These institutions were not the products of abstract reason; rather, they were the fruits of empiricism plus a long run of good luck.

The Norman Conquest marks the point of departure in any examination of the development of English liberty. The Norman vassals were too weak to resist the king unless they allied themselves with the Anglo-Saxon squires in the country and the small merchants and traders in the towns. This they did, and out of the alliance emerged in time the British Parliament. In France, on the other hand, the king owned few estates and had to depend upon the urban bourgeoisie for the funds and forces needed to secure his realm against his vassals. Feudal England, starting with a nearly absolute monarchy, had developed by the eighteenth century into a limited, parliamentary monarchy. In France, events followed the reverse course; a kingdom possessing little power had by the seventeenth century become an absolute monarchy.

A characteristic institution of all feudal regimes was the Grand Council, composed of the lord's principal vassals, charged with advising him on all matters of importance and aiding him in the administration of justice. The council had to give its consent whenever the king needed funds in excess of those he could draw from his own lands.

At the beginning of the thirteenth century, King John (Lackland), at war with the King of France and under the ban of the Church, found himself in open conflict with his English barons. Taking advantage of his defeat at Bouvines (1214), they wrested from him the first in a series of contracts—the Magna Carta of June 15, 1215. Although their object was to enforce recognition of their feudal privileges, the charter benefited all future generations by establishing three of the great principles of modern law:

1. That there are rights belonging to the English people which the king must respect. If he does not, his subjects may rebel. This is the basic principle of all constitutional governments.

2. That "no free man shall be taken or imprisoned or disseized or exiled or in any way destroyed, nor will we go upon him, or send upon him except by lawful judgment of his peers or by the law of the land." [3] This is the principle which would be developed in the *Habeas Corpus* Bill of 1679 and the Bill of Rights of 1689, acts which guaranteed individual liberties then unavailable in any country of Continental Europe: the right to be neither arrested nor detained without the prompt intervention of a judicial sentence, the right to a jury trial, and the right to free speech.

3. That "There shall be no taxation without repre-

sentation." This is the principle for which the American colonies would contend in the eighteenth century.

By the end of the century, Britain's Grand Council had come to be known as the Parliament. The Model Parliament of 1295 was composed of five elements: barons, bishops, knights, delegates from the towns, and representatives of the clergy. The clergy eventually withdrew, preferring to vote their contributions in their own assemblies, while the other four separated into two groups according to their special interests. From these emerged the House of Lords, the House of Commons, and the bicameral system.

Given the Crown's continuous need for funds, and the appearance of a propertied urban middle class during the fourteenth century, one might have expected parliamentarianism on the Continent to develop as in Norman England. But this did not happen. Rather than submit to the tutelage of the Cortes, the kings of Spain preferred to enter upon a policy of persecution directed against two minority groups, the Jews and the Moors, a course of action which enabled them to seize the properties of these wealthy minorities and thus make themselves financially independent of their subjects. In France, the division of the Estates General into three orders voting separately condemned all three to impotence and twice, in 1358 and again in 1484, prevented the realization of a parliamentary monarchy. From 1484 on, the French monarchy advanced steadily along the path of absolutism which would lead at last to the Revolution of 1789.

In England the Revolution of 1688 marked the triumph of Parliament. Following the flight of James II, the "Convention" gave the crown to William of Orange and imposed upon him the Bill of Rights, which still constitutes that country's most extensive constitutional safeguard. The Bill declared that the king could not suspend the application of existing laws, levy taxes or maintain an army in time of peace without the consent of Parliament, and that the Parliament had to be convoked frequently. No one was to be harassed for addressing petitions to the king, a right further developed in 1707 when it was enacted that the king could neither refuse bills submitted to him by the Parliament nor modify existing laws through administrative order. Thereafter the legislative power rested entirely with the Parliament.

From earliest times, the English kings had surrounded themselves with private counselors, through whom they exercised their powers. Under Charles I and Charles II, the term "cabinet" came to be applied to this small group of royal confidants. After the emergence of the two-party system (the Whigs and the Tories), the kings regularly chose their cabinets from the members of the majority party.

When the first of the German Hanoverians, George I, mounted the throne, he ceased to attend the meetings of the cabinet, whose members spoke a language he did not understand. The cabinet exercised all of the executive powers and regarded itself as responsible only to Parliament. The king "reigned but did not rule." The cabinet's position was further strengthened by substituting the principle of the collective responsibility of the group of ministers under the leadership of the prime minister for the old practice of individual impeachment. This assured the stability of the government until such time as a serious conflict forced the ministers and the deputies to seek a mandate from the people.

More and more groups were included in the electorate in the course of the nineteenth century, and universal suffrage was realized early in the twentieth. While preserving the appearances of monarchy, England had in effect become a parliamentary democracy.

The system is completed and balanced by the independent position of the judiciary. Honored, well paid, freed from the need to worry about their advancement, the judges are assured of their autonomy. Armed with the *habeas corpus,* the power to forbid any arrest or arbitrary detention, protected from political pressures and the popular passions of the moment, the English judge is the implacable custodian of the laws and the guarantor of British liberties.

FROM THE HISTORIC RIGHTS OF ENGLISHMEN TO THE NATURAL RIGHTS OF MAN

British liberties found expression in a series of historic acts which introduced certain practical and effective procedures, notably: the power of the courts to issue an order to bring an arrested person before them, a procedure which protected a person from inquisitorial practices; penal responsibility of officers and agents of the police; financial responsibility of examining magistrates.

As British concepts and practices passed from England to America and to France, they kept their content but freed themselves from accidental and historical factors, taking on a more universal character.

In the American case, the transformation was prompted by the fact that the British Crown had broken its contract with its colonies. Consequently, the colonials no longer invoked "the rights of English citizens," but the universal "natural-rights" concept that stems from Greco-Roman times.[4] It is to Locke's *Second Treatise on Government* (1688) that we owe its orderly development and expression. Political society, Locke argued, is the result of an original contract among a number of people who agree to surrender a part of their original liberties in order to defend such essential rights as the ownership of private property through the combined strength of the social body. Popular consent, he held, is the only legitimate basis for government; hence no government could be absolute and legitimate. The legislative power is the primary power; the executive can function only in conformity to it. In this fashion Locke legitimized the Glorious Revolution of 1688 and the investiture of the House of Orange. Blackstone, writing in the tradition of Locke, said:

The rights themselves (Magna Carta, Bill of Rights, Petition) . . . consist in a number of private immunities; which will appear, from what has been premised, to be indeed no other than either that *residuum* of natural liberty, which is not required by the laws of society to be sacrificed to public convenience; or else those civil privileges, which society hath engaged to provide, in lieu of the natural liberties so given up by the individual.[5]

Such were the principles which inspired the American Declaration of Independence:

We hold these truths to be self-evident, that all men are created equal, that they are endowed by their Creator with certain inalienable rights, that among these are Life, Liberty and the Pursuit of Happiness. That to secure these rights, Governments are instituted among men, deriving their just powers from the consent of the governed.

These same ideas reappeared in the Articles of Confederation of 1777 and in the first ten amendments to the Constitution, ratified in 1791.

The American concept of democracy thus rests on the Lockean idea of a social contract, designed to protect the inalienable rights of the individual, and not as Hobbes and Rousseau defined it, as a total surrender to the community by each individual of *all* his rights.

In seeking an institutional framework for these principles, the American Founding Fathers developed an essentially new form of government: the federal system. The American Constitution is the result of a contract or pact made between the member states and a central government superimposed over them. The Constitution safeguards the rights of the member states by prohibiting the central government from trespassing on matters reserved exclusively to them. It does more than define the competence of the central government and the state governments; it limits the competence of each in its dealings with individuals and local groups, by listing individual and public liberties with which the legislatures may not interfere. The central government controls and directs only a few of the activities of the American people; groups of individuals and local authorities, the towns and counties, play the striking roles which so impressed de Tocqueville in the 1830's. The governments of the member states, local collectivities and private groups make decentralization of power a reality. De Tocqueville pointed this out on almost every page of his book, *Democracy in America:* whoever urges centralization urges despotism, and whoever defends decentralization defends liberty.

The American Constitution achieved an authentic separation of powers. The Congress, the President and the courts are independent bodies, each clothed with separate delegations of power. Each body is controlled by the other two, which prevent its powers from becoming oppressive. Because of the bicameral principle, the House of Representatives, elected in proportion to population, serves as a counterweight to the Senate, in which the several states are accorded equal weight. The executive serves as a check on the Senate and the House; the judiciary checks the executive and legislative powers. The states counterbalance the central government.

All these powers are subordinated and limited in turn by the Constitution. It is the expression of the original will of the people, and is the supreme law of the land. The judges in each of the fifty states are bound by it, and this has produced the most remarkable creation of American jurisprudence: the jurisdictional and constitutional control of the laws and acts of government. The Supreme Court by majority vote can declare unconstitutional any law it judges contrary to the rights of the member states, or to the rights of individuals as enumerated in the first ten amendments.

When one considers how a constitution drafted by a group of country gentlemen for four million colonials has adapted itself with a few minor changes to the requirements of the most industrialized country in the world with a population of 200 million, one is forced to ask if it does not still represent the most certain guarantee of liberty yet provided any nation.

The American revolution spread like a tidal wave. It swept over Ireland and Great Britain, crossed the channel to the United Provinces, Belgium and Switzerland, only to be crushed by conservative forces. Finally it burst upon France and from there it spread to all parts of Europe.

THE FRENCH REVOLUTION

A few months before the American Declaration of Independence, the Parlement of Paris solemnly declared that "any system which, under the mantle of humanity and charity, sought to establish among men in a well-governed monarchy an equality of duties and to obliterate social distinctions, would soon lead to disorders which would destroy that society." [6]

Fourteen years later, a financial crisis forced Louis XVI to convoke the Estates General. By proclaiming themselves a National Assembly, the members of the Third Estate in effect transferred sovereignty from the king to the nation, as represented by the elected deputies. Almost overnight the Assembly abolished the whole edifice of the *ancien régime,* and in the Declaration of the Rights of Man and Citizen proclaimed that the object of political institutions

is to protect the natural, inalienable and sacred rights of man which are liberty, property, security and resistance to oppression;

that the principle of sovereignty resides in the nation; that law is
the expression of the general will and should be equal for all; that
all citizens are equally eligible to all dignities, offices and public employments; that liberty consists in the right to do anything
which does not harm another; that no one may be accused, arrested or otherwise detained except in cases determined by law;
that no one may be punished except by virtue of a law passed
and promulgated prior to the act; that all citizens may talk,
write and print freely, subject to liability for abuses of liberty in
accordance with the provisions of law.

The Assembly in effect established a liberal monarchy
based on the separation of powers, an elected judiciary, and
an electoral system more liberal than that of Great Britain.
Two out of three adult males enjoyed the right to vote. The
new regime was regarded as "a social contract" between the
citizens and the king, who had renounced his claim to absolute sovereignty in order to become the guardian of the
constitution. This constitutional monarchy was greeted with
almost unanimous enthusiasm and appeared to warrant the
high hopes it had aroused. Yet those hopes, for reasons that
were in part accidental and in part inherent in the system,
were soon to be disappointed.

The suppression of the *ancien régime* had produced something approaching anarchy. Taxes were not collected; the
public credit was shattered; a serious food shortage grew
steadily worse. Administrative reform had transformed the
local authorities into elected bodies; more than 20,000 locally
elected officials could neither read nor write. To compensate
for their incompetence and to meet the perils arising on every
side, the Assembly assumed executive powers in addition to
its legislative authority. Stripped of his prerogatives and his
role as moderator, torn between his duty as guardian of the
constitution and his religious scruples concerning the civil
constitution for the clergy, Louis XVI could find no other
solution than flight. His capture brought on the republican

agitation. The Paris Commune controlled the streets, terrorized an Assembly composed of men with little experience in public affairs, and in effect ruled the country. To get out of its internal difficulties and to establish national unity, the Girondist Ministry declared war against Austria. The state of war led to the "terror" and that in turn led to Napoleon and the Empire.

More serious than these "accidental" causes for the failure of the Revolution to realize the expectations it aroused were certain structural defects.

The Fathers of the American Constitution held that the sovereign people had expressed their will in the vote for the Constitution. In their eyes this Constitution became the fundamental law to which all governing powers were subordinated. Neither the Congress nor the Administration could pretend to embody the plenitude of sovereignty. The power of the judges to pass on the constitutionality of laws voted by the Congress and of acts of the Administration assured respect for the Constitution.

The authors of the French Constitution held quite different views. They believed the people by an election had transferred their sovereignty to a legislative body which possessed this sovereignty in all its plenitude and not as a delegated and subordinated power. It was an absolute sovereignty acknowledging no power higher than itself, a power so complete that it could change methods of election at will and rewrite the Constitution itself. Limitations on the constitutionality of laws were always rejected as a denial of the general will which had expressed itself by a majority vote of the representatives of the nation.

The outcome of the American conception was the supremacy of the Constitution; the outcome of the French conception was the supremacy of the Parlement. The latter has proved to be a disastrous conception.

That France has had nineteen constitutions since 1789

shows that the French have not succeeded in creating the appropriate institutional framework for the principles they have so eloquently proclaimed. They have never realized a true balance of powers and have therefore been condemned to oscillate between parliamentary and executive omnipotence.[7]

Thus the omnipotence of the Assembly gave way to the omnipotence of Napoleon. The Corsican appeared to be the very negation of the revolution which was to set men free. Yet his military forays overthrew the old regimes throughout Europe, in a chainlike sequence of revolutions extending from the Low Countries and the Rhineland until they reached and overthrew governments as far distant as the Near East and South America. To the princes of Europe, Napoleon seemed to be the booted soldier of the revolution. They defeated it temporarily in 1815. Its flames were rekindled in 1820, in 1830 and again in 1848. It marked a new era in human history. A new type of government, different from the authoritarian governments of the past, had come to occupy the center of the stage: a government chosen by the governed and dedicated to assuring to all men the right to life, liberty and the pursuit of happiness.

THE LIBERAL CONCEPTION OF THE STATE

Man's long struggle to free himself from the tyranny of the omnipotent state had finally resulted in the recognition that human beings have certain irreducible rights. But whence come these rights? From the Creator, some say; from reason, according to Cicero and the theorists of the law of nations; from experience, say the utilitarians. But whether they come from God, from nature or experience, the end result is the same: the liberal conception of the state. At the end of the eighteenth century, the jurists were as one in proclaiming that individuals are obliged to surrender to the state *no more* than the minimum of their liberties necessary to protect the rest.

If the record of history demonstrated that men had enjoyed more leisure and more opportunities for self-improvement in planned societies than in societies based on liberal principles, then no religious beliefs or philosophical convictions could have overthrown them. But the historical record proves exactly the reverse. The theory of natural rights both explains and justifies the permanent drives which flow spontaneously from the natural aspirations of men living in social groups. Respect for these rights on the historical record is a necessary precondition for the prosperity and happiness of societies.

A society is capable of peaceful resolution of its internal conflicts to the degree that it leaves individuals free to venture, to create, and to decide for themselves the best use of their energies and resources; to the degree that it is open, it facilitates the movement of skills and talents, discourages the state from undertaking functions which individuals and private associations can best perform for themselves. A society is happy, in a word, to the degree that it leaves individuals free to handle their own affairs within limits defined by law in consideration of the general welfare.

XIV

THE ACHIEVEMENT
OF FREEDOM OF THOUGHT

Foremost among the liberties for which the people of the West have shed their blood is freedom of opinion—the right to express one's views in word or writing, exempt from harassment and persecution. Without this right, there can be no such thing as free inquiry, and little likelihood of discovery or invention. Without this right, democratic government is inconceivable, since the existence of a political opposition implies the liberty of expression. Without this right, there can be no public spirit, no possibility of being informed, of discussing public policies. There can be no citizens, only subjects; there can be no progress, only stagnation.

The battle for liberty of thought has assumed various forms according to the times. During the Middle Ages and the beginnings of the modern era, its objective was religious tolerance. With the secularization of the state and the advent of representative government, the struggle focused increasingly on freedom of information, freedom of speech and freedom of the press.

The bitterest conflicts and most ruthless battles have concerned religious liberty. Antagonists do not fight over a theorem of geometry, because its validity can be demonstrated to any thoughtful mind. People rarely fight over a demonstrable fact, even though it lends itself to a number of interpretations. It is in areas where conclusive demonstration and the evidence of the senses cannot help us that disputes are most acrimonious, and precisely because the commonly accepted criteria for settling disputes are lacking. Thus it is with beliefs of a religious, philosophical and metaphysical nature.

RELIGIOUS TOLERANCE IN ANTIQUITY

Religion, as the Latin word *religio* ("to tie together") indicates, was originally the tie that bound primitive societies together. The Aryan family was formed around the worship of the hearthstone. The tribe was built around a common god—a tribal deity. The city gathered around the worship of its protecting divinities. The Roman Empire was founded on the cult of Rome and the genius of Augustus. To reject the cult of the gods of the hearth, of the tribe, of the city and of the state was to be more than renegade; it was to be treasonous. Piety and patriotism were inextricably bound together.

The more a community was menaced, the more implacable became religious intolerance. The terrible sentence of ancient Jewish law, which the Christians would invoke so often in their internal wars and their massacres of the unbelievers, was the most heartless manifestation of this intolerance: "If thy brother, the son of thy mother, or thy son, or thy daughter, or the wife of thy bosom, or they friend, which is as thy own soul, entice thee secretly, saying Let us go and serve other gods, . . . thou shalt not consent unto him, . . . neither shalt thou spare, neither shalt thou conceal him: But thou shalt surely kill him, thine hand shall be the first upon him to put him to death." [1] Religious intolerance is especially characteristic of monotheistic societies which recognize no god but their own, and which tend to combine civil and political power with religious power, and place it in the hands of a priestly caste. Intolerance was less apparent in the polytheistic societies of antiquity because there was less need for it. Postulating the existence of a number of gods, they naturally admit the legitimacy of various cults. They also tend to identify the deities of one cult with those of another despite differences in names, a tendency known as syncretism. The Greeks recognized their gods in other nations' gods. Roman conquests made this tendency politically necessary. The cults of the conquered could not be abolished. The gods of Rome became the gods of the new citizens and the gods of the new citizens were adopted by the Eternal City.[2] Paganism was a vast collection of divergent faiths.

This fusion of gods into a single pantheon was the easier because the religions of antiquity were purely ritualistic. They involved neither creed nor dogma; everyone was free to interpret the meaning of religion for himself. There was, for example, a Stoic rendering of mythology, alongside a very different Neoplatonic interpretation. Religions promising salvation were accepted as a form of eternal insurance; if there were an afterlife, the more religions one subscribed to, the better his chances of getting there. In Rome the highest religious functions were discharged by laymen who regarded them, for the most part, as simple acts of administration.

The exception was the religion of the Jews. The God of Israel was a jealous God who admitted no other gods besides Himself. Moreover, His laws formed a code of civil conduct. They raised a "barrier of observances" between Jews and Gentiles, which led the Gentiles to accuse them of misanthropy. The Empire recognized the Jewish people as a nation and placed them alongside various other national cults; in keeping with the notion of religious coexistence, Judaism was a *religio licita,* a tolerated religion. This was not enough for the Jews. They demanded many privileges, such as the right to be ruled by their own magistrates, and to be exempt from participation in the imperial cult.

The Christians, on the other hand, constituted neither a nation nor an ethnic group. They refused to accept public office, to serve in the army, to appear as witnesses in courts of law, to do anything which required the taking of oaths. Rejecting the imperial cult, therefore, constituted a kind of running sabotage throughout the Empire; and this precisely at a time when its existence was threatened by barbarians pressing in on every frontier. The persecutions of the Christians were motivated by social and political considerations, not by doctrinal prejudice, and were for the most part local and sporadic. The number who died for their faith in the course of three centuries was less than the number of Protestants executed by Charles V in the Low Countries alone in the sixteenth century. Tertullian (ca. 225 A.D.), the Carthagenian Christian theologian, expressed the prevailing Christian reaction to these persecutions: "It is impious to deprive man of his freedom in matters of religious belief, to prevent him from choosing the divinity of his choice. No man and no god wants forced service." [3] The case for religious freedom has never been better put.

CHRISTIANITY AND RELIGIOUS INTOLERANCE

The situation was very different after the triumph of Christianity. The new religion, in contrast with the purely ritualistic religions of antiquity, preached salvation through a faith based on a divine Word, as revealed in the Scriptures and confirmed by the tradition, which remained in the jealous control of the Church. Acceptance of Church dogma, as formulated by the Church Fathers and the councils, became the condition *sine qua non* for salvation. "Let whosoever would be saved guard above all else the Catholic faith. If he does not preserve it entire and inviolate, his damnation is certain." So proclaimed the Athanasian Creed.

Judaism, withdrawing inward after the destruction of the

Temple of Jerusalem, addressed itself only to the chosen people. Christianity saw as its mission the conversion of the entire world. From that time on the terrible sentence of the Ancient Law was applied to all people: "And the man who will do presumptuously, and will not harken unto the priest that standeth to minister there before the Lord thy God, or unto the judge, even that man shall die: and thou shalt put away the evil from Israel." [4]

The pagan Roman emperors had persecuted the Christians for civil disobedience; the Christian emperors would persecute the infidels for the crime of heresy. Judaism would remain the only tolerated religion, to play the role of a witness to Christianity, on the condition of remaining in a servile position. Infidels were to be converted by persuasion or force; heretics were to be cut off from the community of the faithful by excommunication, and from society of the living by death inflicted through the secular arm of government. The humiliating position allowed the Jews would produce ghettos, pogroms, massive expulsions and forced conversions.

The excommunication of the heretics lit the fires of the Inquisition. The persecution of Christians by Christians, the quarrels of sects and wars of religion, spread throughout the world a physical and ideological violence that antiquity had never known. Shortly after the triumph of Christianity, Ammianus Marcellinus wrote, "Wild beasts are not more ferocious enemies of man than Christians are enemies of Christians." [5]

The Church hypocritically reconciled its duty not to shed blood with its duty to exterminate heretics by turning this salutary task over to the temporal authorities. This is what it did in the thirteenth century in the extermination of the Cathari and the Albigensi, sterilizing a civilization and depriving France of the privilege of anticipating the Renaissance before Italy. It is what the Church did again in the sixteenth century, when it provoked the terrible Hussite wars by its torturing of John Huss and Jerome of Prague. Other Protestants met similar fates later in that century in the fires of the Inquisition.[6]

If it was the genius of the West to dare defy the ancient curse, and taste of the fruits of the tree of knowledge, we must nevertheless recognize that Christianity did its best to destroy the tree. Christianity feared the spirit of inquiry and doubt, rejected the power of reason, and hated findings of the natural sciences as threats to belief in her miracles. "The triumph of Christianity," as Condorcet pointed out, "was the signal for the complete decadence of the sciences, as well as of philosophy." [7]

It might have been expected that the Reformation, in proclaiming the principle of free inquiry, would introduce the idea and practice of religious tolerance. In fact, it did no such thing. Luther liberated religion from the Roman curia only to deliver it to the secular princes, in accordance with the formula *cujus regio, ejus religio*—the religion of the ruler determines the religion of the ruled. The dispute between the Church and the Empire had at least one fortunate consequence: it made clear that there was in fact a distinction between temporal and spiritual matters. The new force of Protestantism tended to blur this distinction.

The King of England broke with Rome in order to establish an Anglican Church under his exclusive control. In Hungary, a folk saying grew, "Faith in Calvinism is faith in Hungary." The Protestant princes, happy to seize the properties of the Church, sought everywhere to establish national communions. Even Gallic France, then fully committed to Rome, did not stand apart from the movement which was leading to the emergence of the great modern states, a movement which ended the ecumenical community which the Christianity of the Middle Ages had represented.

In 1839 Pope Gregory XVI characterized liberty of conscience as "a madness." It was not until the 1965 session of Vatican Council II that the Church renounced anathemas and, "as an hypothesis," finally accepted the concept of liberty of conscience, based upon respect for the human person. The Catholic Church no longer imposes, it proposes; it does not condemn, it invites discussion. It addresses itself to all people as a friend and an ally, seeking to contribute to the solution of human problems by appealing to the fundamental moral requirements of social living.

THE STRUGGLES FOR TOLERANCE AND THE NEUTRALITY OF THE STATE

It was the stalemate in the wars of religion which brought about tolerance in religious matters, in the modest form of the liberty to err. Since neither the Huguenots nor the Papists had succeeded in destroying the other, they had to resign themselves to living in the same world together. In time it became clear that a pluralistic society was viable, and that, in the presence of a variety of faiths, the state could best assure their peaceful coexistence by remaining neutral.

This is what Sébastien Castalion argued at Geneva against Calvin, with a courage as admirable as his logic. In his *Should Heretics Be Persecuted?* (1554), he showed to what absurdities an affirmative answer to this question led. One and the same man would be declared orthodox in one city and a heretic in a neighboring city! [8] A century later Pierre Bayle dared speak on behalf of tolerance in his *Dictionnaire historique et critique* (1695–97), and John Locke, in his carefully argued *A Letter Concerning Tolerance,* insisted that "neither pagan, nor mahometan, nor jew, ought to be excluded from the civil rights of the commonwealth because of his religion. The gospel commands no such thing. The church 'which judgeth not those that are without' (I Cor. v. 11) wants it not." [9]

In the eighteenth century, Montesquieu, Voltaire and the German Lessing, among others, propagated the ideas of Bayle and Locke.[10] It was Voltaire above all who led the battle. The persecutions of Calas, Sirven and de la Barre in the 1760's forced him into a position of leadership among the philosophers: "Come, brave Diderot, fearless d'Alembert, fall upon the fanatics and the rogues. . . . This is not the time for pleasantries. Sweet words are out of place when massacres are afoot. Is this the country of philosophy and gentle living? It is the country of St. Bartholomew!" [11] For two decades Voltaire inundated Europe with his letters, petitions, diatribes, dictionaries, novels, verses and plays. His was the clear voice of reason; he fought tirelessly for tolerance, justice, freedom of the press, and for the abolition of feudal privileges; he denounced the abuses of the corporations and guilds; he urged the reform and unification of civil and criminal law, and public assistance for the needy. From every corner of Europe, the most enlightened men made pilgrimages to the patriarch of Ferney, who had been exiled because of his beliefs. Before his death he returned to his beloved Paris, there to receive glorification from a grateful people.

Statesmen, convinced that political unity is impossible without religious unity, were slow to embrace these new ideas. In France, where the wars of religion had made men sick of massacres, the Edict of Nantes (1598) constituted, despite many restrictions, a timid affirmation of the new right on which would be built all modern societies: the differentiation of civil law from religious law. This demarcation of the rights of the state from the rights of conscience was a first step toward the secularization of the state. But with the revival of religious quarrels during the seventeenth century, religious intolerance took on new violence and led to the revocation of the Edict of Nantes in 1685. Catholic education for all children was made mandatory; 50,000 families fled France. It was not until the French Revolution that the Declaration of the Rights of Man and Citizen proclaimed: "No one shall be molested for his opinions, religious or otherwise, provided their manifestation does not disturb the public order as established by law."

In England, the Act of Toleration (1689) was far from meeting the tests posed in Locke's *Letter Concerning Tolerance*. It excluded from public offices all Catholics, Unitarians, Jews, infidels and Dissenters. Locke himself, unlike Bayle, was intolerant of atheists, and though he demanded tolerance for Presbyterians, Anabaptists, Quakers and Separatists, he did not dare include Unitarians. The right to vote and to take seats in Parliament, despite promises made to the Irish at the time of the Act of Union (1800), was not granted to Catholics until 1829, and it was not until 1860 that Jews were accorded the full rights of British citizenship.

Although the quest for religious freedom was the determining motive of many of the 750,000 Presbyterians, Quakers, Baptists and Lutherans who emigrated to North America between 1600 and 1700, it is nonetheless true that most of the state constitutions drafted after the Declaration of Independence excluded from public office and denied the vote to Catholics, Deists and Jews. Membership in these confessions meant the loss of one's civil rights. With the passing of the first amendment in 1791, the principle was established that the Congress could make no law "respecting an establishment of religion, or prohibiting the free exercise thereof." This was the principle of the freedom of religion and of the neutrality of the state which was to become the law of the great democratic nations of modern times after so many centuries of futile religious strife.

THE ACHIEVEMENT OF FREEDOM OF SPEECH AND OF THE PRESS

Religious liberty is only one aspect, although it is the one which has involved the shedding of the most blood, of a larger liberty: liberty of thought. As modern states became more secularized, the struggle for liberty of thought became increasingly a struggle for freedom of speech and of the press.

In 1644 John Milton published an attack on a law of the previous year which had suppressed the freedom of the press. His book, the *Areopagitica,* addressed to the House of Lords and the House of Commons, argued the dangers and damages of such a law. Protestants feared the law as a reintroduction of the practices of the Roman curia and the Inquisition, which had been the main target of their opposition. Only by allowing people to read bad books as well as good, Milton asserted, does the human spirit learn to distinguish between good and evil, to absorb the good and reject the bad. A censor can be wrong and can condemn as false what tomorrow will be recognized as true. Milton recalled the trial of Galileo, whom he had visited when he was "old and a prisoner of the Inquisition because he had wished to think otherwise about the field of astronomy than the Franciscan and Dominican censors." [12]

In France, the censorship of books goes back to the time of Francis I (ca. 1540). It was exercised originally by the University of Paris and its Faculty of Theology. Under Louis XIII (ca. 1640), the university lost most of its authority in this area to the Chancellery, which we would call today the Ministry of Justice. The Chancellor named the royal censors, whose written approval was required before a book could be published. But alongside their written authorizations developed tacit authorizations, and publication was possible under the king's seal. All these permissions could be revoked by decree of the Parlement as the court of last resort.

The *Encyclopédie,* a work destined to assure the triumph of the philosophical spirit in its struggle against tradition and authority, was published under Diderot's editorship, and despite the harassment of this confused censorship. The work was repeatedly interrupted. The king's privilege was secured in 1746, suspended for eighteen months following the appearance of the first two volumes under the attacks of the Jesuits and Jansenists, and suspended again in 1757, this time by the Parlement. Finally, after eight years, Diderot overcame the obstacles thrown in his path and was able, under a tacit permission to resume publication, to complete the last volume in 1772. In the midst of this crisis Malesherbes, as Director General of the Library, wrote his celebrated memoir in defense of freedom of the press.

If we forbid the publication of error, we block the path to truth because new truths are always regarded for a time as errors and are rejected as such by those in authority. . . . The freedom of the press to discuss public affairs is one of the most powerful supports of the liberty of a republic, since it is what gives to each citizen the means of warning the nation of the abuses of authority. . . .[13]

In 1763, Diderot wrote his *Memoir on the Liberty of the Press.* He traced the history of censorship, denounced its excesses, revealed its absurdities, and proposed solutions based on the great principles of political philosophy set forth in the *Encyclopédie.* Without liberty of the press, he argued, there could be no progress of the spirit. The sciences, technologies, the fine arts, man's knowledge of himself and his world can progress only if the principles, the means and the methods underlying them are perpetually rediscovered. This rediscovery presupposes the continuous circulation of ideas, hypotheses and information from one man to another, one country to another, and one century to another.

Sire, you can hedge our frontiers with soldiers, arm them with bayonettes, charge them with keeping out dangerous books, and yet these books, . . . will slip between their legs and leap over their heads and reach us just the same. Cite me, I beg of you, one of these dangerous works which, whether printed secretly abroad or within the realm, has not within four months become as common as any book approved by the censor. . . . How many times would publishers and authors of privileged works, had they dared, not have said to the magistrates and police, "Gentlemen, please, a little decree condemning me to be whipped and burned at the bottom of your great stairway." [14]

But freedom of the press had to wait for the Revolution. Article 11 of the Declaration of the Rights of Man and Citizen of 1798 said: "Free communication of thought and opinion is one of the most precious of the rights of man. Every citizen may therefore speak, write and print freely, on his own responsibility for abuse of this liberty in cases determined by law." The same first amendment to the Constitution of the United States of America that guaranteed religious liberty denied to the Congress authority to enact laws "abridging the freedom of speech, or of the press, or the right of the people peaceably to assemble, and to petition the Government for a redress of grievances."

Freedom of speech and of the press is one of the fundamental guarantees of individual liberty. It is essential if the opposition is to be heard, if public opinion is to be informed, if discussion is to replace violence, if a government of men is to be guided by the salutary light kindled by the peaceful confrontation of opposing opinions. Censorship, advanced authorization, warnings, suspensions, and confiscations of books by simple administrative rulings have always been the weapons of weak governments fearful of facing opposition. A government which is strong because it is free welcomes opposition; indeed, it will not hesitate to institutionalize opposition by paying the leader of the loyal opposition, as is done in Great Britain.

Denial of freedom of the press is an expression of hatred

for the human spirit. Beaten, repressed, rejected, this spirit, which alone makes peaceful progress possible, may disappear for a time, but it will always reemerge. In Victor Hugo's words, "It is this human spirit which, for as long as it has existed, has transformed societies and governments in accordance with a law ever more in accord with reason." [15] One might say that Western civilization is a civilization of dialogue which extends to minorities and to the opposition the right to express themselves. Without tolerance, confrontation among ideas is not possible; without such confrontation, there is no critical intelligence. Without critical intelligence, science gives place to dogma and fanaticism. Liberty of thought is at the very foundation of Western civilization.

XV

THE TAKE-OFF OF THE WEST

Three revolutions, economic, industrial and political, combined to launch the West on a rapid course of development which set it apart from the rest of the world.

The substitution of liberal democracies for monarchies by divine right, the attainment of equality before the law, free access to occupations—these changes spurred the spirit of enterprise, opened careers to individual talents, and released energies which asked only the chance to exert themselves. Thanks to the spread of education, the selective play of competition raised up a new species, aggressive, productive and technically inventive, quite different from the cleric, and the nobleman prevented by the traditions of his class from engaging in money-making activities. The nations of the West became more dynamic, and in the exuberance of their vitality, imperialistic. By commerce, colonization, conquest and the contagion of example, they progressively transformed the world.

In this expansion, however, the West had to overcome certain handicaps. A market economy, as Adam Smith defined it, was the only system capable of permitting the industrial revolution to achieve its full effects. Before this could happen, it was necessary to create the appropriate institutional framework. First of all it was necessary to abolish all the commercial and craft regulations inherited from the Middle Ages, as well as the mercantilist restrictions of the

Tudor period in England and the period of Louis XIV in France. These restrictions were designed to encourage domestic industry, but they in fact granted monopolistic privileges at home and abroad.

THE ABOLITION OF THE CORPORATIONS

The medieval corporations, with their control over processes of manufacturing, blocked all innovation. In 1643, the British Privy Council, not content with simply refusing a patent for a revolutionary knitting machine, ordered its destruction. In France, enforcement of the prohibition on the import of printed calicos cost the lives of thousands of people. In the town of Valenciennes alone, 77 people were hanged, 55 broken on the rack, and 631 sent to the galleys for the crime of trading in these articles. "The regulations are so rigorous," Grimm wrote in 1765, "that officials and clerks at the ports of entry may legally strip any lady venturing to wear in public a gown made of linen." [1] With a view to curbing the innovating spirit in the textile industry, Colbert issued a decree requiring that cloth made in Dijon and Selangez had to contain 1,408 threads, including the selvages, those made in Auxerre and Avallon 1,375 threads, and those of Chatillon 1,261. In England there were laws against weaving cloth which did not meet precise specifications as to dimensions and weights, against drying processes which might stretch the threads, and against cleaning processes which served to stiffen the cloth.

To enforce these complicated regulations, England, France, and most of the other European countries, maintained an army of inspectors. The regulations were enforced by trustees, justices of the peace and other officials armed with the power to impose heavy penalties, ranging from fines to the seizure of the goods themselves. From the death of Colbert (1683) to the beginning of the Seven Years' War (1756), the French government published more than a thousand regulations of this sort, some running to as many as two hundred articles. The industries created by royal initiative, administered by public authorities, or subsidized by the state were frank monopolies and were widely denounced by well-informed people like Arthur Young as harmful to the industries themselves.

The corporations, and the monopolies created by the state, had the same crippling effect on invention and innovation as did antique slavery. For long centuries technical ideas accumulated but were unable to find practical application. When the barricades were suddenly swept away in the late eighteenth and early nineteenth centuries, it is not surprising, as Professor Roepke pointed out, that industrial development proceeded at a revolutionary pace.[2]

The Industrial Revolution required the freeing of commerce and industry from the regulations of the corporations and monopolies. This was done in France, after Turgot's abortive attempt of 1774, by the Constituent Assembly, whose members had read or otherwise become familiar with that catechism of emancipation, Smith's *Wealth of Nations.* "As of April 1st" (1791), the law declared, "a citizen will be free to exercise any profession or practice any occupation." In England it was not until 1813 that the Statute of Artificers of 1563, which regulated the number of workers and apprentices, was repealed. The field was free for the operation of market forces which, despite many interferences and tribulations, would in the course of a century and a half transform the world.

THE RISE OF THE PROLETARIAT AS A PROTEST AGAINST THE MARKET ECONOMY

The determination to free commerce and production from private-interest coalitions led the Constituent Assembly to vote a law, named after its author, Le Chapelier, prohibiting professional associations. Any coalition of private citizens formed to protect their common interests was declared "unconstitutional, a threat to individual liberty and in violation of the Declaration of the Rights of Man." In England, workers had begun to form unions as early as 1750. But traditional English law likened such associations to conspiracies, and a law of 1799 forbade them.

Abandoned to his own resources, without moral or material support, uprooted from his rural background by the development of factory production, forbidden to gather with his fellows to defend his interests, menaced with unemployment by the periodic crises of overproduction provoked by the rapid introduction of machines, regulated by the Le Chapelier law in France and a corresponding law in Britain, the worker became a proletarian.

Michelet has described very vividly how mechanization dehumanized the worker. The craftsman at his bench could dream at times; his was the comfortable workshop described by Hans Sachs and the songs of the Lollards. In the new factories, on the contrary "the machine tolerates no dreaming, no distractions. Should you wish to slow the tempo of your work for a time and then speed it up, you cannot. It sets your pace. A human being, a person of flesh and blood whose vitality varies from hour to hour, must conform to the invariability of this creation of iron." Michelet closed on a note of deep pessimism. "The emptiness of the spirit, the absence of any intellectual interest, this is one of the main causes for the degradation of men working in factories. A work which requires neither strength nor skill, which never calls for thought! Nothing, nothing and always nothing. No human being can endure this!" [3]

Day in, day out, amid noise and dust, the worker, fatigued by hours of unremitting toil, led a gloomy existence, chained to a monotonous task, devoid of personal significance.

Villermé in his *Report,* Disraeli in *Sybil,* and Zola in *L'As-somoir* described the frightful conditions under which children, women, miners and workers generally had to labor. These conditions were not so much due to the laws against association, and to the *laissez faire, laissez passer* of the economists, as to the introduction of machines and the exodus from the countryside into the cities.

The proletarian hurled accusations at a society which alienated him, a society in which he felt no interest. Unaware of the improvement of his material condition, he was conscious only of his new wants, which mounted in step with the technical progress that made their fulfillment possible. The concentration of workers around factories, plants and mines gave them a sense of shared destiny and made them feel that they had interests in common everywhere—with the "damned of the world." Class-consciousness became all the stronger as the working class, and the guilt-ridden bourgeoisie, produced orators and agitators who, following the advice of Ferdinand Lassalle, "taught people how unhappy they were."

The working class, deprived of religious comfort by the philosophers of the eighteenth century and the scholars of the nineteenth, became demanding. At the end of his *Mémoires d'outre tombe,* Chateaubriand drew up the balance sheet for his times and predicted: "The masses, having lost their faith in a life hereafter, will demand a paradise on this earth; that is to say, a sharing of fortunes by the expropriation of the wealthy, and an equality for all." [4]

The condition of the proletariat constituted a new challenge to Western civilization, a challenge which the optimistic economists of the eighteenth century had not foreseen. This problem became more serious when two English economists, Thomas Malthus and David Ricardo, argued that there was no remedy for the condition of the proletariat, that the misery of some was the condition for the prosperity of others.

According to Malthus, or more accurately, according to his popularizers,[5] population inevitably increases faster than the means of subsistence, and equilibrium can be restored only by wars, famines and epidemics, or by voluntary restrictions on births by the working classes. For Ricardo, an increase in population required the cultivation of lands of steadily diminishing fertility. Since the prices of agricultural products had to cover costs on the marginal, or least fertile, lands in use, and since these prices were the same for all producers, owners of superior land necessarily received an extra income, or rent, whose continued increase corresponded to the gradual increase in output. The "laws" of Malthus and Ricardo rested, not on man's avarice, but on the stinginess of nature against which legislative interventions could do nothing.

From these pessimistic considerations Karl Marx concluded that capitalism, based on private property and private enterprise, could not endure. The increasing pauperization of the workers, and the growing accumulation of capital under the control of an ever smaller number of capitalists, had to culminate in a revolutionary situation which would end the inherent contradictions arising out of the collective methods of production and the individualistic methods of distribution. The "red night" of revolution would come when the proletarians seized power and liquidated the exploiters. The dictatorship of the proletariat would be followed by the emergence of a classless society based on the common ownership of the instruments of production, economic planning, and the withering away of that instrument of oppression, the state.

THE MARXIAN ANSWER TO THE CHALLENGE
PRESENTED BY THE PROLETARIAN CONDITION

The challenge of the proletarian condition aroused a variety of reactions, ranging from peaceful utopias through reform proposals to violent revolution.

Utopian proposals associated with the names of Babeuf, Saint-Simon, Fourier, Cabet, Owen and Proudhon have all left some traces on modern societies. Only the anarchists, the theoreticians of violence, left nothing constructive. It was otherwise with Marxism, which grounded itself in an inclusive philosophy of history.

Marxism rests on the conviction that capitalism cannot eliminate the proletarian condition through its own inherent development, that only revolutionary violence can resolve the system's inherent contradictions. This conviction was derived by Marx from an analysis of the modes of production of his own times and of the then prevailing conditions of the working classes. Industry and commerce were directed to satisfying the needs of the propertied classes; peasants and workers stood largely outside this circle of exchange and felt they were denied its benefits. On the basis of this analysis, Marx ventured a number of predictions.

He predicted, first of all, an increasing concentration of capital. The development of machines and the elimination of the less skilled through competition would result, he said, in the progressive swallowing up of the little capitalists by the middle-sized ones, and of the middle-sized ones by the big ones. This process would go on until capital was concentrated in the hands of a small group of giant industries.

This concentration of capital would in turn bring about the increasing pauperization of the masses. The productive processes would be necessarily directed to satisfying the needs of an ever-dwindling clientele, and this would inevitably bring about recurring crises of overproduction. These crises would cause unemployment, creating a surplus of unemployed workers on the labor market whose very presence would drive wages down.

The capitalist class, as a result of the pauperization of the masses, could not but increase the number of its enemies. It would thus find itself in the paradoxical position of "having to support its own slaves, instead of being supported by them." The revolution would come when the capitalists could no longer provide the masses with the miserable subsistence which made their slavery tolerable. When this happened, "the masses will expropriate the few usurpers," in contrast to the past in which the few expropriated the many.

History has refuted Marx. The concentration of business, in the sectors where it has occurred, has been accompanied by the democratization of capital through corporate share-holding by people of modest means. At the time Marx wrote, the modern corporation was beginning to make it possible for small savers to become part owners in businesses of great size. In the United States, the majority of the shares in "big business" are held by salaried workers.

Nor has the wage earner been pauperized. To find markets for mass-produced goods, business had to turn inward, after its conquest of foreign markets, and seek its buyers among the working classes. Thanks to a policy of paying high wages and encouraging wage earners to buy stocks, it succeeded. The worker became doubly interested, as a wage earner and an owner, in the enterprise employing him, and therefore in capitalism itself.

A further consequence of the high-wage policy has been the discrediting of the rhetoric of "class struggle." Wages have ceased to be at the subsistence level. The curve of wages has departed further and further from the curve of prices. In France, real wages (measured against those of 1910 as the base year) rose from 53.8 in 1830 to 89.5 in 1890, and to 106.7 in 1911. Since then the rate of increase has been even greater. In the United States (with 1913 the base year), the index stood at over 248 in 1955. Nor has unemployment increased as predicted. On the contrary, countries experiencing rapid growth have faced a situation of overfull employment.

Marx, and Lenin after him, envisioned the progressive disappearance of the state and its instruments of oppression, the army and the police. Exactly the opposite has occurred. In the Communist countries the coercive apparatus of the state has enormously increased and inevitably so. To realize an authoritatively determined plan of economic development, the monetary constraints imposed by the price mechanism of the market had to be replaced by harsh legal penalties, including forced labor, and even the death penalty for acts which in a market economy would be no more than misdemeanors. Production, distribution and consumption all have been minutely regulated, tasks which require an enormous bureaucracy under the control and supervision of the Communist Party.

Marx's proletarian revolution was supposed to produce a classless society. But, as Milovan Djilas has shown in his book *The New Class,* we have witnessed not the coming of "the Republic of Equals" but the appearance of a new class, the bureaucrats. This truly privileged group, well remunerated in money and services, enjoys the exclusive right, based upon the monopoly power of a single political party, to distribute the national income as it sees fit, to fix wages and salaries, to direct economic life, and to control the disposition of the nation's accumulated wealth.

The market economy transformed peasants and day laborers into consumers whose freedom to spend their incomes as they desired informed producers in competitive markets, through the plebiscite of prices, of the relative urgency of their needs and the nature of their tastes and preferences. Producers had to shape their plans accordingly. A planned economy imposes its priorities with little or no heed to the wishes of consumers. Consumer-goods industries have been sacrificed in favor of the heavy industries, of armament and rivalry in outer space. In this sense, the market economy is a far truer expression of *economic democracy* than any authoritatively planned economy because in it the needs and tastes of consumers determine the direction which investment and consequently production will take. Profits are a sign of the ability of producers to read these needs and tastes correctly. In a planned economy the consumer is a serf; in a competitive market economy he is a king.

MODERN CAPITALISM'S ANSWER TO THE CHALLENGE PRESENTED BY THE PROLETARIAN CONDITION

The nations which remained faithful to the market chose the middle way between utopia and violence, the way of reform. To combat pauperism and resolve "the social question," the public powers intervened. Alongside a civil code "designed for an ideal citizen, born a foundling and dying a bachelor," there developed a network of social legislation protecting against accidents, unemployment, sickness and old age.

The liberty to bargain collectively was recognized in England in 1825. The right to form private associations was granted in France in 1864, and the legality of collective bargaining was recognized in 1881. A series of innovations changed the relations between labor and capital: collective conventions; worker representation on committees; varieties of profit-sharing arrangements; co-management (in certain branches of German industry); worker participation in ownership through stock purchases; guaranteed wages; reduced working hours; professional training; and public commitments to maintain full employment. Enterprises tended to become true working communities in which the wage earner understood the significance of his work and shared in its successes.

In the spring of 1914 Henry Ford announced that he would henceworth pay higher wages than anyone else, that no one would receive less than $5.00 a day, that hours of labor would be shorter than in any other industry, that he would sell his automobiles for less and make higher profits than any of his competitors—and all this without reliance on the banks. Point by point he carried out his program.

His method was simple. It rested on the economies of mass production, which lower unit costs by reducing the amount of overhead or general costs taken up by each unit produced. This lowering of the cost of production was to be reflected in lower selling prices and higher wages, thus transforming his own workers into customers. Ford even reduced the work week to five days to give his workers two successive days in which to enjoy his popular car.

To the *profit motive* was added the *wage motive*, or, in more general terms, reliance on a generalized purchasing power, from which the profits of the business would come as a by-product. Ford envisaged owners, workers and the buying public becoming parts of a single community. He saw profits as the by-products of a collective service well performed.

What I have here described and call Fordism has also been called neocapitalism. Whatever its name, it has given a total refutation of the Marxian predictions. Fordism democratized capital by making wage earners stockholders and thus at once consumers and property owners. In the United States, where the wage earner lives the life of a European bourgeois, the proletarian condition has practically disappeared. The capitalism of the American captains of industry—the Rockefellers, the Carnegies, the Morgans and the Mellons—has become a "peoples' capitalism" which is realizing the goals of socialism without socialists.

THE TRANSFORMATION OF THE WORLD BY THE MARKET ECONOMY

The market economy has changed the face of the globe. The relatively free circulation of capital, goods, techniques, technicians and workers has brought within its orbit distant lands; it has made idle spaces productive; it has equipped the whole planet. In a single century the population of Europe rose threefold, that of the United States tenfold; in five generations the broad masses in the West have experienced a more rapid rise in their material way of life than in all the centuries separating them from the Greeks.

The opening of foreign markets and the development of colonies represented the great accomplishment of nineteenth-century economic liberalism. In an atlas of one hundred years ago the interiors of continents were represented in vague outline and labeled "unknown lands." The exploration of North America had hardly started. The immense valley of the Amazon, the Andes and the Pampas are shown only by trails recorded by a few explorers. Central Africa was as mysterious as Australia; Siberia was a desert; China and Japan were enigmas. The white race was almost entirely contained in the tiny European peninsula, like an appendix of Asia. And then the change began. Investment banks, inundated with savings, underwrote loans designed to develop the resources of new countries. A few weeks after the banks acted in Europe, speedy packboats unloaded machines and building materials on savage shores. Railroads pushed into virgin lands, carrying the artifacts of Europe and bringing back the native products. Earnings from these exchanges encouraged the formation of new groups of investors, and the opening of new countries. On the eve of World War I, there were no more "unknown lands" to be found in the atlases of the day.

What Ford had accomplished in America occurred in other nations of the West, demonstrating that the interests of producers, consumers and workers could be reconciled. "Thanks to science, it is possible to make products at less cost, with raw materials which cost more, with labor which is better paid and capital better remunerated, and with larger profits for the entrepreneur." [6]

Aristotle had scoffingly declared that slavery would disappear when shuttles could run by themselves; until then, civilization would depend upon slavery. In order to raise the shining marble of the Parthenon onto the Acropolis, in order to allow philosophers to discuss at their banquets the subtle problems which preoccupied the Greek spirit from the time of Parmenides, thousands of human beings had to live the lives of dumb beasts in the quarries of the Pentelikon, on the stony and scorched fields of Attica, in the Laurion mines, and in the slave prisons of Pireus. The best Christianity could do was to transform the slave into a serf and a moral person; the best the French Revolution could do was to clothe him with the inalienable rights of a man and a citizen.

The skilled worker of today—in terms of his food, clothing, entertainment and cultural formation—lives a life a master craftsman of the days of Louis XIV could not have imagined. The peasant of Western Europe and the farmer of North America bear no resemblance whatever to La Bruyère's savage beast, or to Rousseau's tiller of the soil. In five generations the working man has gained more material comforts than during the previous twenty-five centuries.

This prodigious improvement went on throughout the whole of the nineteenth century and the first half of the twentieth, in spite of two world wars. It is revealed in the massive increase not only of wealth but also of population in the industrialized and semi-industrialized countries of Europe (from 187 million in 1800 to 600 million in 1960). The population increase was due in part to progress in medicine and public hygiene, but primarily to the economic take-off following upon the invention of the machine. A few statistics make this abundantly clear.

The Industrial Revolution of the eighteenth century was based on coal and steam. In 1800 the world's annual production of coal was about 15 million tons; by 1860 it had reached 132 million tons. In 1900 it stood at 701 million tons and fifty years later at 1,454 million, equivalent to 11,632 million megawatt hours. But thermal energy is only one among many forms of energy. The world's production of commercial energy rose from 1.1 billion megawatt hours in 1860 to 6.1 billion in 1900, to 21 billion in 1950, thus annually putting at man's service an increasing number of mechanical slaves.

Around 1800 the cost of food in most countries absorbed 85 to 90 percent of the average income of the people. This proportion has fallen to less than 50 percent in the industrialized countries. Consequently the share of agriculture in the national incomes of such countries has considerably declined. It represented 40 percent in the United States in 1800, no more than 8 percent in 1950, and the percentage of the population of working age engaged in agriculture fell from 75 percent to 9 percent. In France, which is still agricultural, the decline was from 55 percent in 1860 to 30 percent in 1950. As a country develops, its active population tends to pass from the primary sector (the extractive industries) into the secondary sector (the manufacturing industries), and from the secondary into the tertiary sector (the service industries). From 1850 to 1935, the percentage of workers in the United States moved from 32 percent in the primary sector to 9 percent, from 19 percent to 25 percent in the secondary, and from 42 to 60 percent in the tertiary sector. One hundred and fifty years of technical progress doubled per capita food consumption, increased the consumption of manufactured products a hundredfold and services sixfold.

A few mortality figures sum up all of these accomplishments and provide the clearest possible refutation to the objections frequently raised against a technically oriented civilization: life expectancy increased from 25 years in Western Europe at the beginning of the eighteenth century to 72 years today for men, and to 74 years for women; infant mortality per 1,000 births has fallen from about 250 to around 20; the average length of marriage has risen from 17 years to 39; and the average age of the child at the death of its first parent is

44 today as against 14 at the earlier period. Family life and the whole social structure have been transformed.

This economic revolution, in combination with the Industrial Revolution, has opened up a new era in human history, an era in which men, living in technical societies, strive ceaselessly to improve the human condition through science and its applications.

XVI

WESTERN CIVILIZATION AND
THE CIVILIZATIONS OF THE EAST

Western civilization evolved from a special way of looking at nature and at life. Its uniqueness lies in its success in breaking free from taboos, prohibitions, and ancestral customs which could not justify themselves by social utility or provable beneficence; in mastering the surrounding world by understanding its laws; in its unceasing search for ways to improve the material conditions of human life in general, while respecting the essential dignity of each and every individual.

THE INCOMPATIBILITY OF TRADITIONAL CHINESE
MENTALITY WITH THE IDEA OF PROGRESS

At the outset everything seemed to indicate that China would enjoy a scientific and technological development similar to, if not superior to, that of the West.

Chinese mathematical thought was profoundly arithmetic and algebraic, but unlike the Greek mind it never developed an axiomatic and deductive geometry.[1] It was content with the measurement of surfaces and volumes. In astronomy the Chinese made very precise observations with the aid of remarkable instruments.

Nonetheless, failing to conceive the idea of natural law, the Chinese did not develop the fundamental sciences until after the arrival of the missionaries from the West. They pictured the world as one vast organism with all its parts intimately and sympathetically related one to another. In their view, the task of science was to discover these multiple interdependencies, such as those which bind the microcosm (man) to the macrocosm (the universe). Nature was a symbolism to be deciphered, and for this purpose a number of pseudosciences were constructed—numerology, astrology, geomancy and physiognamy—all of which were incompatible with the discovery of physical laws. The Chinese never rose to the abstract idea of a homogeneous and isotropic space such as Euclid conceived and could express in geometric terms. Their physics remained caught in the metaphysics of Yin and Yang, the five elements, and their symbolic affinities. Hence their science never got beyond the pre-Galileo level. Joseph Needham, perhaps the greatest authority on Chinese science, observes:

When we say that modern science developed only in Europe and only in the time of Galileo at the end of the Renaissance, we are trying to say that then and then only were laid the foundations of the structure of the natural sciences as we know them today; that is to say, the application to nature of mathematical hypotheses, the full understanding and systematic use of the experimental method, the distinction between primary and secondary qualities, the geometrization of space and the acceptance of a mechanical model of reality.[2]

The Chinese were an industrious and practical people. They excelled in map-making and meteorology; they created the science of seismography and were pioneers in civil and hydraulic engineering. They mastered the art of casting fifteen centuries before Europeans did and were among the first to use coal. To their ingenuity the world owes the first mechanical clocks with escapements and balance wheels; powder, which they used for fireworks long before making hand grenades for the wars of the Sungs in the twelfth century; the compass; paper; silk; and printing with movable letters. Nevertheless, they did not apply this inventiveness to their industry, which remained essentially unchanged over the two thousand years between the accession of the Han and the fall of the Manchu dynasty.

Why not? Because the Chinese were interested in a different set of values from those which preoccupied the West. Instead of trying to dominate nature, the Chinese sought to adjust themselves to a cosmic environment, natural and human. The two essential problems of concern to the Chinese were the search for good government and the art of finding contentment in the midst of poverty and adversity.

The first problem concerned the philosopher and teacher Confucius, who died in 479 B.C. Confucius regarded man as essentially social, and he took as his personal mission the saving of a world which seemed to him to be in full decadence. His solution involved the restoration of five essential virtues: good manners (*li*), distributive justice (*yi*), kindness, filial piety and wisdom.

Confucianism, at once a theory of government and a theory of ethics, produced strong patterns of social ritualism, and the written language of China helped maintain this conformity. The immobility of words, formed of monosyllables, tended to stereotype thought and to freeze social life. Confucius and his school recognized this when they insisted that the remedy for the disorders of the times was to be found in the "rectification of words." To assure good government, everything had to be identified by its true name, and everyone had to conduct himself in accordance with the correct designation of his function. The incorrect use of words was a semantic sin leading to social disorder. It was important, therefore, that public functionaries be recruited by examinations based on their knowledge of classical books (*King*), named and written in an ancient language very different from that in contemporary use, and requiring the mastery of tens of thousands of characters. For two thousand years the institution of the Mandarin attracted the best minds into the services of an administration whose primary concern was to maintain a static social order, in harmony with and dependent upon an unchanging cosmic order.

Taoism, anterior to Confucianism, stands in sharp contrast to it. However, its results were even worse, for Taoism negated logic and encouraged evasion. Lao-tse, who died in 521 B.C., attributed all misfortunes to man's departure from the state of nature when he tried to control his destiny. The social virtues praised by Confucius—justice, good manners, wisdom and kindness—were regarded as conventions and obstacles to the natural order of things and deserving only of contempt. Laws merely multiplied the number of thieves and bandits. For Confucius, the good sovereign was one who did everything possible for his people; for Lao-tse, the best sovereign was one who saw that he could do nothing and let matters take a natural course. Man must return to his original state of innocence. Through asceticism, life could be prolonged; immortality itself was possible for him who could absorb himself in the ecstasy of Tao, an indescribable reality which was everywhere, which had no definite limits and was the origin and supreme law of things.

Such mentalities made progress of the Western sort a theoretical as well as a practical impossibility. Prior to the arrival of Westerners, China, like Japan, was a closed society which regarded itself as perfect, as having nothing to learn from foreigners. When King George III of England proposed to the Emperor Ch'ien Lung (1735–95) the establishment of diplomatic and commercial relations between the two countries, the Son of Heaven replied:

As to your request to be allowed to send one of your nationals to be accredited to my Heavenly Court in order to control the commerce of your country with China, this request is contrary to all the usages of my dynasty and cannot be considered. . . . Our ceremonies and our code of laws differ so completely from yours that, even though your representative could acquire the rudiments of our civilization, you would not be able to translate our manners and customs to your alien soil. . . . Master of a vast world, I have only one end in view, to maintain a perfect government and to fulfill the duties of state. I attach no value to strange and ingenious objects and expect no benefits from the goods made in your country.[3]

Withdrawn behind an intellectual and moral "Chinese Wall," the Middle Empire could not develop until the arrival of the barbarians, the European and American "devils."

THE INCOMPATIBILITY OF THE TRADITIONAL HINDU MENTALITY WITH THE IDEA OF PROGRESS

Some fifteen hundred years before Christ, a brilliant civilization of the Indus Valley was submerged by the invasions of the Vedic Aryans. The religious hymns and sacrificial rites of the conquering peoples were written in Sanskrit over a period of 500 years, ending in 1000 B.C., constituting the Vedas. The Vedas reveal a high level of accomplishment in astronomy and mathematics. Technical improvements proceeded at very different paces among the many groups making up the ethnic mosaic of India. The most remarkable were those involving work in metals, lacquers and textiles, and in the psychosomatic techniques of Yoga. Unhappily, following the expulsion of Buddhism from India by the violent Brahma reaction which constituted Hinduism, scientific progress declined and the torch passed into Arab hands.

After an honorable start, India failed to attain through its own efforts the level of technical and scientific competence of the West. As with China, the failure was traceable to a different way of looking at the world.

East and West started with the same pessimistic assumptions: the human condition is precarious, painful and fleeting. Theognis of Megara (ca. 640 B.C.), Simonides of Chios (ca. 460 B.C.) and the Greek tragedies all passed judgments on existence fully as bleak as Buddha's. But the responses were different. In the West, they suggested actions to improve the situation; in India, evasion. Western man sought to remedy the misery of his condition by mastery of the world; the Hindu sought to escape the world by mastery of self, of the internal life of the spirit. The Western mind believed in the reality of the external world and undertook to impose upon it the power of man's will; the Hindu regarded the external world and the idea of Ego as illusory, and sought to submerge personality in the quietude of the impersonal and timeless "Self."

From the Himalayas to Ceylon, people of all degrees of cultivation accepted the same transcendent law (Karma) of eternal transmigration of souls (samsara) and the rewarding of acts over the course of a series of existences. Religion and philosophy together preached the nothingness of the individual, the illusory vanity (maya) of material things.[4]

The highest wisdom was to escape from the wheel of rebirths by the technique of depersonalization, to be had through the mastery of knowledge of Samkhya or the psychosomatic methods of deliverance of the Yoga. The purpose in both cases was to enter into an ecstatic fusion with the Absolute (Brahma), who, in his positive form, is Being itself, and in his negative form is Nothingness, the Nirvana.

To this metaphysics, with its denial of the wish to live, must be added a compartmentalization of Hindu society which prevented the invigorating circulation of elites that alone can keep a society healthy. Hindu culture was built up from successive waves of conquest which left the aborigines at the bottom and the latest conquerors at the top. Since the caste into which one was born was believed to be the result of all the acts committed in preceding existences, escape was inconceivable. The pariah accepted his fate as the expiation of faults committed in his previous existence, and as the condition for enjoying a better life in some future reincarnation. Thus the caste system enclosed the individual in a sort of social jail. He had to marry within his caste; he could break bread only with members of his caste; acceptance of so much as a handful of rice from a person of an inferior caste brought in its train such a corruption as to lead to expulsion from one's own caste. There was no possibility of rising from one caste to another; there was no "social ladder" to climb. Since the position of the pariah was metaphysically merited, nothing was done prior to 1950 to improve his condition.[5]

The habit of contrasting the crude materialism of the West with the spiritualism of the East needs to be revised. The great Asiatic civilizations developed in a pre-logical era; the mind groped for truth through intuition, symbol, magic and mysticism. It was irrational. It refused to see the external world as an autonomous reality capable of being shaped and adapted through an understanding of its laws.

The West, thanks to Greek genius, succeeded in rising to the level of rational thought, founded on respect for a principle of no concern to the Oriental mind, the principle of contradiction. By associating the Hellenic *Logos* with the Christian *Word* and the Roman *Law*, Europe realized a synthesis which, despite many tribulations, is still the most miraculous accomplishment of the human adventure.

HOW ARABIC CIVILIZATION WAS FETTERED BY ISLAM

From the eighth to the twelfth century the Islamic Empire, made up of many peoples, extending from the Pyrenees to the limits of China, preserved Hellenic science, enriched it with borrowings from Persia, India and even China, and finally transmitted it during the twelfth and thirteenth centuries to the Latin West. Over a period of five centuries, during which darkness settled over the West, the home of civilization was in the Near East and in Spain; its language was Arabic and its sun was the sun of Allah.

As long as Islam was in the hands of the Arab race, however, there was no intellectual development involving a concern for matters of this world. It was different once the Persians gained the ascendency, and the Abbaside caliphs supplanted the Ommiads at Damascus. The Abbasides established their new capital at Baghdad and made it the center of the civilized world, while a prince of the Ommiads escaped to Spain, where he established a realm which was practically independent.

The brilliant caliphs who followed one another at Baghdad—al-Mansur, Harun al-Rashid and Marmoun the Great, contemporaries of the Carolingians—respected the external rituals of the religion of which they were the chiefs, but, like the popes of the Renaissance, they interested themselves in many other matters. Surrounded by Persians, Syrians, Nestorians, Jews and free-thinkers of every race, they showed themselves as tolerant as their priests, the imams, permitted. They patronized open debates on such subjects as the respective merits of different religions judged by the light of reason. Marmoun sent his emissaries to Greece and India in search of manuscripts; he employed the Christian Nestorians to translate the works of Aristotle, Euclid, Archimedes, Apollonius, Hippocrates and Galen. In 830 he founded an academy with a splendid library, called the House of Knowledge, and made Baghdad the intellectual center of the world.[6]

Following the collapse of the Abbasidian Empire, the "Arabian Miracle" spread to Aleppo, to Cairo where the Fatimids founded the University of al-Azar, and across the straits to Cordova, whose three hundred mosques were called "the pearls of the world" and whose glory eventually rivaled Baghdad's. The brilliant rays of this Asiatic civilization penetrated deep into France, Italy and Sicily. Arabic and Jewish doctors from Spain settled at Salerno and Montpellier. Arabic medicine was taught at Venice and Padua down to the sixteenth century.

During the second half of the eleventh century, the political power of the Arabs declined with the taking of Baghdad by the Seljuk Turks, the reconquering of Aragon, Toledo and Palermo by the Christians and the entry into Jerusalem by the Crusaders. The caliphate of Cordova broke into many small states with Seville, Granada and Malaga as their capitals.

In the twelfth century the Near East experienced a new Harun al-Rashid in the person of Saladin, who conquered Jerusalem in 1187, and a new Mansur in his nephew, the Egyptian Sultan Malik al-Kamil. The latter established a sort of permanent center of scientific studies to which the scholarly free-thinker and Emperor of the Two Sicilies, Frederick II, addressed himself. And meantime, to the West, the Almohades in Spain inaugurated a new golden age which survived in Cairo until the Mamelukes brought Egypt under Turkish domination, and in Baghdad until its capture by the Mongol hordes in 1258.

Expelled from Europe by the Christians, driven from Asia by the Mongols, subjected to the Turks in Egypt, the Arabs lost contact with the Persians, the Syrians, the Christians and the Jews whose presence had played a vitalizing role in Arab culture. Thrown back upon themselves, they sank into a long torpor from which they were not aroused until the nineteenth century and the coming of the peoples of the West.

How is this sleep of Islam to be explained? It was due to the fact that the Parsees, the Christians, the Jews and the pagans who accepted the religion of Islam had done so more to be free from various onerous taxes than from any real conversion. The scholars who constituted the "Arab Miracle" were for the most part Syrians, Persians and Spaniards, peoples who were not Arab by blood, and had nothing of the Arab spirit. Once these alien elements were eliminated, the Islamic masses again fell under the yoke of their fanatical imams. From 1200 on, a theological reaction swept through Islam. There were no longer philosophers—the word itself became synonymous with "infidel"—and only occasionally was there a scholar like the fourteenth-century historian, Ibn-Khaldun. The Turks, devoid of the critical and probing spirit, imposed their heavy yoke on Islam; and Islam, returning to its sources, paralyzed inquiry with a formula which brooked no answer: *Allah aalam,* God knows best what is.

The traditionalism of Islam is incompatible with the spirit of inquiry and the idea of progress. For the Muslim, all truth worth knowing is contained in the Koran, at once a dogma and a code of faith, whose prescriptions regulate the smallest details of life. Whatever happens is the will of Allah. All is preordained; the only thing to do is to submit without complaint. This fatalism is destructive of effort, of any manifestation of personal will. It expresses the atavistic resignation of the nomad before the emptiness of the desert. Belief in another life, full of sensuous delights, of houris and fresh meadows, consoles the faithful for present tribulations. This mentality rules out restlessness, dissatisfaction with self, that constant drive to improve which is the moral mainspring of the internal life of Western man.

The Muslim recites prayers, but makes no orisons; he feels no sense of guilt and expresses no *mea culpa.* From the moment he satisfies the fundamental prescription of the Koran, which is to believe in the one God and his Prophet, Muhammed, he is at peace with himself. There results a quietism which bears the outward appearance of a noble serenity, but excludes all effort to improve the human condition. Since Allah has made man's home what it is, why try to improve it by inventions which border on impiety and contribute nothing to man's salvation? Why maintain the Roman aqueducts at Carthage? Better to settle where a natural spring wells up from the earth, as at Kairouan. The industrious Jew creates canals to water the Negev and converts it into a land of smiling fields and prosperous towns. The Arab, shepherding his sheep on these same fields, turns it again into a desert.

The religion of Islam rules out intellectual curiosity. Omar, burning the books at the Library of Alexandria to warm the Moorish baths, is only a legend, but the words attributed to him are full of significance: "If these books say the same things the Koran says, they are useless; if they say anything else they are false and should be destroyed."

The Islam of today, under the impact of Western civilization, seeks to become part of the modern world. Mohammed Abdoh, Rector of el-Aztar, who died in 1905, tried to rid Islam of its scholastic trappings and to open it to the scientific spirit and the idea of progress. Mustapha Kemal, before he could modernize Turkey in the 1920's, had to separate the caliphate from the state, adopt a civil code based on Switzerland's, abolish the religious brotherhoods, emancipate women and forbid the wearing of the fez and the turban. In Egypt, members of a sect called the Muslim Brotherhood had to be brought before courts of law, imprisoned and even hanged for refusing to make the least concessions to the modern spirit. They justified their refusal with this profession: "Allah is our ideal; the Prophet is our chief, and the Koran is our Constitution."

XVII

THE RISKS OF PROGRESS

Some sixty years ago in the capital of a church in Gotha a document was found which had been placed there in 1784. In it appeared this passage:

Our days are the happiest of the eighteenth century. Emperors, kings, princes descend benevolently from their awe-inspiring height, forsake splendor and pomp, and become their . . . people's father, friend and confidant. Religion emerges in its divine glory from the tattered clerical gown. Enlightenment makes giant strides. . . . Religious hatred and intolerance are disappearing, humanity and freedom of thought gain the upper hand. The arts and sciences prosper, and our eyes look deep into nature's workshop. Artisans, like artists, approach perfection, useful knowledge germinates in all estates. This is a faithful picture of our times. Do not look down on us haughtily if you have attained to greater heights and can see further than we do; mindful of our record, acknowledge how much our courage and strength have raised and supported your position. Do likewise for your successors and be happy.[1]

THE EIGHTEENTH CENTURY'S BELIEF IN
CONTINUOUS PROGRESS

This jubilant declaration reflects the generous optimism of the Enlightenment. To the intellectuals of that day it seemed that humanity, having outgrown both the swaddling clothes and the fables of its infancy, had exchanged the garments of its adolescence for the vestments of maturity.

In France, the century of the Port Royal school gave way to the century of the Encyclopedists. Belief in the original goodness of man replaced the Jansenist idea of human corruption due to original sin. Salvation through expertise replaced salvation through grace. By gaining knowledge of the laws of the universe, men felt that they had made themselves masters and possessors of nature.

Men believed human nature could be perfected through the power of education over the individual, and the power of legislation over the nation. Helvetius wrote his widely read book, *L'Esprit* (1758), to show that "spirit, genius and virtue are the products of education," not gifts of nature. "From the humblest Alpine shepherd," he stated, "we can shape at will a Newton or a Lycurgus." [2] In the same vein, Madame Roland declared that "the infinite differences found in men are due almost entirely to education." [3]

"If the laws are good a people's morals will be good; they will be bad if the laws are bad," said Diderot.[4] And Helvetius insisted that the vices of a people were the product of bad laws. "The lawmaker can if he will create heroes, geniuses and men of honor." [5] Condorcet was convinced that a good law was good for all people everywhere, "exactly as a theorem in geometry is true to all minds." [6] In this spirit Rousseau drafted constitutions for Corsica and Poland without feeling any need to visit either nation.

This belief in the inevitability of progress was an exciting and delightful dream. Like the goddess Hope, blindfolded with lyre in hand, as we see her depicted on the celebrated canvas of Burne-Jones, she leads humanity straight into a glorious tomorrow.

Unfortunately, the intellectuals of the eighteenth century and the ideologues of the Revolution had vastly simplified the nature of the problem. They believed that the spirit of an infant at birth was like a blank piece of paper that education could write upon what it would. This was a denial of any inherited psychological traits which would create initial inequalities. They were convinced that institutions which worked well in one society could be transferred in their entirety to other societies with equally good results. This ignored differences in the mentalities and degrees of maturity of different ethnic groups. In seeking to force people to be free, the Revolution unleashed twenty-three years of war, aroused a spirit of rampant nationalism, and substituted for the cosmopolitan Europe of the Enlightenment a divided continent of chauvinistic states. In place of the limited wars of kings, national conscription substituted wars of extermination. In place of monarchies which were limited by established orders, universal suffrage substituted the omnipotence of irresponsible assemblies which, by pretending to act in the name of the sovereign people, used them and oppressed them.

By its universal call to arms, capital levies, "assignats," fiat issues of paper money, nationalizations and confiscations, price fixing, one-party system, laws against suspects, and systematic use of terror as a method of government, the Convention (1792–95) realized the first totalitarian government in the history of Europe. The wars of the Revolution, which were intended to bring peace to all the world, and the wars of the empire, which were to produce a peaceful and united Europe, called forth the Holy Alliance, the Restoration, and a principle, that of nationality, destined to spawn the fratricidal wars of the nineteenth and twentieth centuries.

HOW PROGRESS DRAWS FROM ITSELF
NEW CHALLENGES

Progress cannot be taken for granted. Nor is it continuous. Each advance seems to confront humanity with new challenges which force it to new efforts to outdo itself and accomplish the impossible.

The past of Western civilization provides a permanent record of this struggle. Slavery was no doubt necessary in the beginning so that a few people could have the leisure to think, meditate, discuss, investigate and create the disinterested sciences such as the axiomatic and deductive geometry of the Greeks, their explanatory astronomy, their statics of solids and fluids, the optics and medicine based on clinical observation. But the price was heavy. An exclusively aristocratic conception of knowledge became isolated from the problems of real life. The people at large did not appreciate the utility of a science which did nothing immediate to make their lives easier. They turned to religions which promised rewards in a future life for the sufferings of this one. Through the flood-gates of the Orient such religions poured into the Roman Tiber. The revelation of mysteries beyond human understanding, with their retinues of pseudosciences and magical rites, took precedence over the methods of the true sciences because the latter failed to enlist the mass of slaves and humble people, the *humiliores*. The ancient world perished because its leaders believed with Lucian that the many lived for the sake of the few—*paucis humanum vivit genus.*[7]

It was to the disinherited that Christianity originally addressed itself. It did much to develop a belief in the dignity of man. It lifted the obloquy which lay on manual labor and the mechanical arts. It in large measure fostered concern for social justice. But by making the acceptance of its dogmas the condition of personal salvation, the Church came very close to directing the European civilization of the Middle Ages down the path followed by Islam and India, and therefore to making us miss the narrow path of scientific evolution.

If the Arab world had not saved the scientific heritage of

Greece, and if it had not transmitted that legacy to the West, Europe would not have learned from Greek scholars, and particularly from Archimedes, the art of applying mathematics to the study of natural phenomena. The mathematical physics which we owe to the genius of Kepler, Galileo and Newton might, as in China before the coming of the Europeans, never have seen the light of day.

The Industrial Revolution of the eighteenth century, and the enterprising mentality which accompanied it, nurtured the technical civilization which is one, but only one, of the characteristics of the West. This technical civilization created within itself a new handicap, the proletariat, in response to which many peoples adopted a Marxist viewpoint involving the sacrifice of individual liberty to an economic growth obtained by the dictatorship of a single party and centralized authoritarian government. Fortunately the genius of the West overcame this handicap by mass production and a "people's capitalism."

As progress resolves certain issues it provokes new ones, sometimes even more formidable than those of the past. At least three confront us today.

THE POPULATION EXPLOSION

Progress in medicine and public health has banished the great epidemics of the past, drastically reduced infant mortality and prolonged life expectancy. But in so doing it has raised the threat of over-population, a threat which could cancel out all the accomplishments of technical progress and social reform; and, in creating a conflict between the hungry and the well-fed, could transform class struggles into global conflict between haves and have-nots. Agencies of the United Nations have saved the lives of thousands of children, but for what purpose? If people who otherwise would surely have perished are artificially maintained in a state of undernourishment and pitiful decadence, the total misery of the world has been increased with all its accompanying suffering, despair and degradation.

For most of the underdeveloped countries, the task of raising living standards is extremely difficult. These countries start with an excess population, whereas for the West the growth of population followed and was a consequence of industrial growth. To avoid disaster the leaders of the underdeveloped countries must within the next twenty years use propaganda and education to bring about a reduction of the birth rate, as Japan has successfully done, instead of using the techniques of Western civilization to encourage an increase in population at the expense of the welfare, culture, and happiness of the masses. In the words of Bergson, "If we follow Venus we will beget Mars." [8] To forbid public measures for controlling births is to prepare a genocide in future generations and to make ourselves the accomplices.

THE NUCLEAR EXPLOSION

Recent progress in nuclear physics has been sensational. It has made it possible for man, the modern Prometheus, to ravish the celestial fires in those miniature suns, the atomic reactors. Nuclear reactors will in time supplement the insufficiency of different sorts of power, but our ability to fuse and to split atoms threatens, in the event of war, the survival of man himself.

The threat of nuclear war has had one beneficial effect: the equilibrium of terror has for the moment disarmed the super powers, and exorcised the specter of a third world war. The making of nuclear armament is becoming less costly, however, and this may put this formidable power in the hands of some small fanatical nation, ready to risk everything for what it considers its rights, or of some large nation, prepared to destroy a third to a half of its people to gain the mastery of the world.

The launching of a nuclear war could be the apocalyptic last reaction of a desperate people who have come to prefer the twilight of the gods to a life they find intolerable. It could be due to misunderstanding, to an uncontrolled reflex, to the failure of some control instrument. If it occurs, man will return to the Stone Age in which he fought with flint knives for a bit of raw fish. This sword of Damocles, this apocalyptic danger, can only be averted by an awareness everywhere of the deadliness of the threat. This awareness will come about only when people understand that they all face the same perils, that they are all confronted with the same challenges, that they are all voyagers on the same planet, and that they all face the same destiny.

THE WELFARE STATE

A third danger is less spectacular, but more insidious. As societies grow and become more complex, the state tends to become more grasping and inclusive. To realize the great society of universal comfort, the Welfare State, governments proceed to take from the individual his responsibilities by relieving him of all risks. More than one hundred years ago de Tocqueville described the debilitating effects so clearly as to justify quoting him at length. "I see," he wrote

. . . an innumerable multitude of men all equal and alike, incessantly endeavouring to procure the petty and paltry pleasures with which they glut their lives. . . . Above this race of men stands an immense and tutelary power, which takes upon itself alone to secure their gratifications, and to watch over their fate. That power is absolute, minute, regular, provident and kind. It would be like the authority of a parent, if, like that authority, its object was to prepare men for manhood; but it seeks on the contrary to keep them in perpetual childhood: it is well content that the people should rejoice, provided they think of nothing but rejoicing. For their happiness the government willingly labours, but it chooses to be the sole agent and the only arbiter of that happiness: It provides for their security, foresees and supplies their necessities, facilitates their pleasures, manages their principal concerns, directs their industry, makes rules for their testaments, and divides their inheritances. . . . It covers the whole of social life with a network of petty, complicated rules that are both minute and uniform, through which even men of the greatest originality and the most vigorous temperament cannot force their heads above the crowd. It does not break men's will, but softens, bends and guides it; it seldom enjoins, but often inhibits action; it does not destroy anything, but prevents much being born; it is not at all tyrannical, but it hinders, restrains, enervates, stifles, and stultifies so much that in the end [the] nation is no more than a flock of timid and hardworking animals with the government as its shepherd.[9]

If the price of our security were to be our registration as numbered robots and the abandonment of our personalities to become mere names on registration rolls, if our highest goal were to become the "Babbitt" of Sinclair Lewis, the *señorito satisfait* of Ortega y Gasset, the *uomo qualunque* of the Italians, or the *homme sans denomination* of Musil, we would soon become a decadent species, submerged in uniformity and insipid comfort.

The Welfare State raises the problems of the encroachment of government and the uses of leisure. Where are science and technology leading us? Are they creating a civilization where security and ease will kill the noble restlessness of thought? The answer must be that the abundance technology provides will permit millions to respond to the call of the spirit, a call which in earlier times could be answered by only a small elite.

PROGRESS: THE CHILD OF CHALLENGE

The population explosion, the atomic bomb, and the guaranteed comfort for all are dangers, but they are also opportunities. Historically, the opportunity to overcome such challenges has produced intellectual, social and moral progress.

The peril of overpopulation has given rise to a new ethic: that of family planning, made possible by scientific advances which have substituted voluntary maternity for uncontrolled reproduction. The dignity of women has been increased and the joy of family life enhanced. The unintended children are so often the "unloved ones." Parents are paying greater attention to their responsibilities. What was heretofore nothing more than a work of instinct and chance rises to the level of a voluntary and reasoned act, and consequently a moral act.

The atomic bomb has created an equilibrium of terror. The effects of a nuclear war are estimated in megatons and megadeaths; destruction is calculated by the millions. A menace of this dimension is creating in people everywhere the realization that they are all in the same boat, the little planet earth, which is no more than a grain of sand lost in a vast ocean of worlds. This awareness of a common destiny will eventually result in substituting for the equilibrium of terror an equilibrium deriving from law which will permit the peaceful coexistence of nations. The Treaty of Moscow of August 1963 outlawing nuclear experiments above ground, and Article 9 of the Japanese Constitution denying belligerency as a sovereign right of states, are indicative of this new awareness. If we do not wish to live continuously under the menace of a nuclear war which could be released by accident, by a hysterical act of a visionary head of state, or by a fanatical public opinion, we shall have to come sooner or later to a juridical international order which outlaws the *ultima ratio* of governments as the means for settling international disputes.

The Welfare State in an age of abundance risks creating the by-products of demoralization and decay. Can the average man escape boredom and be happy in an affluent society where his security can be guaranteed by a few hours of light and easy work a day? Actually, modern man may well spend more time on the job than in earlier times if we take account of all the feast days of antiquity, and the holy days of the Middle Ages and the *ancien régimes*. The acceleration of history, the continuous increase in knowledge and the improvements in techniques prevent modern man from living on his past accomplishments; they force him to make constant adjustments. The transfer of the working population from the primary to the secondary and tertiary sectors of the economy is equivalent to continuous promotions. They relieve men of the heavy tasks that exhaust their bodies and spirits, giving them instead lighter tasks which demand more from their brains, less from their muscles.

In a celebrated passage in his *Anti-Duhring*, Friedrich Engels, Marx's close associate, defended slavery as the foundation on which civilization had to be built:

It was slavery that first made possible the division of labor between agriculture and industry on a larger scale, and thereby also Hellenism, the flowering of the ancient world. Without slavery, no Greek state, no Greek art and science; without slavery, no Roman Empire. But without the basis laid by Grecian culture, and the Roman Empire, also no modern Europe.[10]

The great merit of our technical civilization is that it has transformed the worker into a citizen, a free man who can vote and make decisions for himself in a world where intellectual work is becoming steadily more important than physical exertion. The increase in the number of students, the multiplication of schools, colleges, universities and institutes in all countries provide undeniable evidence that culture, a privilege formerly confined to a very few, is becoming available to all. It is in this "cerebralization" of the species that Teilhard de Chardin saw the signs of the emergence of the free spirit from its slavery to the material world. It is here that we may yet find the remedy for that alienation of the worker which Marx regarded as the original sin of capitalist societies.

Thus, in the course of its long ascending evolution, each time humanity crosses a new threshold it faces new responsibilities and new risks. Does this mean that man is condemned eternally to labor like Sisyphus? It is the need to overcome new challenges or to perish that forces man to put forth ever greater efforts. This necessity is less the ransom than the reason for progress, for from danger comes victory, and the greater the danger the greater the triumph.

XVIII

CONCLUSION

A theory of human development propounded by Hegel and
Marx is widely accepted. It holds that through the dialectic
of ideas (Hegel), or the conflict of material forces (Marx),
man's evolution follows a rigorously determined course, ending in a social state on the Prussian model (the Hegelian
ideal) or in a classless society (the Marxian vision). Humanity
is destined, as a result of overcoming internal contradictions,
to go beyond the technical societies of the West. If other
forms of humanity exist on other planets, they too will
undergo similar transformations and arrive at the same
destination.

The historical record refutes any such conception. Among
the different families of primates which began some 500,000
years ago to differentiate themselves from one another, some
never developed beyond savagery or barbarism. Still others,
passing through the Copper, Bronze and Iron ages, succeeded
in evolving higher types of cultures and more complex social
organizations. Human geography provides us with a picture
of all these levels of civilization. Only a few racial groups
passed the threshold of the scientific and industrial revolutions of the seventeenth and eighteenth centuries.

This was not the outcome of any historical imperative.
The rational conception of the world, first formulated by the
genius of the Greek mind, came close to being submerged
in the successive waves of irrationalism which satisfied the

need for the miraculous that lurks, as a survival of the primitive, in every human soul.

To realize the magnitude of Greece's contribution we need only recall her accomplishments between the sixth and the third centuries B.C.—between Thales and his prediction of a solar eclipse in 585 and the death of Archimedes in 212. In less than four centuries, the Greeks had established deductive mathematics, theoretical astronomy, atomism, mechanics, mathematical acoustics, geometric optics, the natural sciences, clinical medicine, positive history and sociology—all guided by scientific methods. The phrase, "This is demonstrated!" found in the works of the Greek mathematicians, constituted the most typical expression of their genius in the domain of learning. In the domain of action, the Greeks created forms of government resting on laws freely discussed and voted upon in popular assemblies. Greece demythologized nature and democratized the life of men in society.

By the time of the Later Roman Empire (254–527), the Greek struggle to introduce rationalism into life had failed. Rome had become a sclerotic, bureaucratized society where everyone was chained to his function—the only escape from which was flight or appeal to the barbarians. Faith had replaced reason. Religions of salvation and false sciences like astrology, manticism, geomancy, and numerology flourished. The last defenders of paganism, such as Porphyry and Julian, believed in demons, oracles, magic and theurgy. The Fathers of the Church condemned the thirst for knowledge as a perilous vanity—a lust due to man's corruption or to the Devil. The critical spirit was crushed. St. Augustine believed that Lucius, the hero of the romance by Apulius, had really been transformed into an ass; and in his *Confessions,* Augustine knew only God and his soul. The great hibernation of thought had begun.

During the Middle Ages, popular preachers praised the *ama nescire,* the love of not knowing. Opposed to them were the Scholastics. These learned doctors reasoned, it is true, but not on the basis of experience. They were concerned exclusively with the evidence of the Scriptures, as interpreted by Church councils; this was revealed knowledge and hence beyond question. The Scholastics manipulated abstract terms; they dealt with universals, untroubled by reference to the world of the senses. They recognized only one kind of mentality, a mentality which sought the truth by appeal not to facts but to words. They regarded conceptual analysis, in which abstract thought and academic vocabulary split things apart, as an expression of ultimate reality. Imposed by the Church and enforced by the secular authorities, Scholasticism exposed Western civilization to the risk of an endless pause.

Between the ·last representatives of Greek science at the end of the third century, and the first representative of modern science in the sixteenth century, between the mathematics of Pappus and the linking work of Vieta, between the synagogue of the first and the isagogue of the second there yawned a hiatus of thirteen centuries. This gap might never have been bridged had it not been for the chance preservation of a few Greek manuscripts which escaped the shipwreck of ancient culture.

China and India, before the arrival of Western visitors, provide us with a picture of civilizations which had been halted in their development by the same forces which affected the Latin West. Despite the promising beginnings described in earlier pages, the only value of knowledge for the Indians was the light it threw on the misery of the human condition, the unreality of appearances and the illusion of personality, destroying attachment to life and leading to deliverance.

Chinese science, before the arrival of the Jesuits, could not develop. The legalists and Confucianists were not interested in nature, and the Taoists scorned reason and logic. Chinese thought never conceived the idea of natural laws capable of mathematical expression. Chinese study of nature was based on direct and superficial observation and aesthetic intuition, rather than on the hypothetical-deductive method of the Greeks and modern scientists, in which hypotheses are tested by experiment.

Thus resurgence of scientific thought in the sixteenth century was almost a miraculous event; it might not have happened, or religious wars might have obliterated it, as the fanaticism of Islamic theologians had obliterated Arabic expressions of science and philosophy. Thanks to the partial rediscovery of Euclid, Apollonius, Archimedes, Heron and Pappus, scientific progress was resumed at the time of the Renaissance, but with a new concern for the reduction of human suffering and the fulfillment of human needs.

The physical sciences and their application brought vast improvements in the human condition. Similarly results were expected of the moral and political sciences. Jean Bodin (d. 1596) insisted that history should guide political policy; it should indicate what to avoid, and what juridical systems and forms of government were best suited to the needs of men. Bodin anticipated Montesquieu, who was to create explanatory sociology through his *Spirit of the Laws*. The physiocrats and Adam Smith founded political economy. They taught the art of mutual enrichment through the division of labor and the complementarity of services. D'Alembert, Condorcet and Laplace developed a "social arithmetic" which enabled legislators to predict consequences, by the application of statistics and probability formulas to collective behavior, and to make effective decisions through what is now called operational research and game theory.

The Promethean spirit of the West is characterized by the progressive and cumulative mastery of the physical and social environment by science and technology. This is not, however, the whole picture. Science and technology are simply means in the service of larger and more important ends. Totalitarian governments have revealed how these means can be used to violate the masses, brainwash them, train them as animals are trained, and make them serve the purposes of ideologues and technocrats. Aldous Huxley in *Brave New World* and George Orwell in *1984* evoke the nightmarish spectacle of societies in which science and technology have reduced human beings through conditioning to the status of robots.

The ends which the power of knowledge should serve are those which come from the prophets of Israel, the sages of Greece, the jurists of Rome, the doctors of the Middle Ages, the humanists of the Renaissance, the Protestant preachers, the theoreticians of the law of nations, the philosophers of the eighteenth century, the socialists and liberals of the nineteenth century. They are the ideals of justice, liberty and solidarity, founded upon respect for the human person whose immanent dignity was proclaimed first by the Stoics and then by Christianity.

Those who doubt that man will continue his triumphant ascent along the path of Western civilization should look to the record of the past. Consider the long upward road he has traveled since his first primitive forebear struck from flint the chips that enabled him to light fires, shape arrows and sharpen carving tools. The domestication of animals, the cultivation of cereals, the shaping of pottery, the building of the first villages, the development of language, the concern for decoration, all helped the neolithic societies of Egypt, Syria, the Indus and the lands around the Mediterranean, to create the first civilized societies. The discovery of copper and bronze, the wheel, the ox cart, the saddle pack, the sailboat, writing, counting and measuring, the flowering of arts and crafts, and specialization in trades combined to produce the urban revolution of the Bronze Age in the Fertile Crescent and in India. The collective accretions of these first communities enabled men to create artificial environments in which they were no longer entirely dependent on nature and its whims.

The forging of the first iron tools by the Hittites made possible the cultivation of barren lands; the discovery of money encouraged commerce and trade, carrying men another long step forward. At this point the Greeks came upon the scene. They transformed the empirical prescriptions of the Orientals into logically related systems; they demythologized nature and sought rational explanations for the wonders around them. Their discovery of self-government started men in a direction that would finally lead to Western civilization.

Christianity, with its condemnation of slavery, its exaltation of work and its insistence on the sacred character of the human person; the Renaissance; the Reformation; the scientific revolution of the seventeenth century; the technical and industrial revolution of the eighteenth; the discovery of the laws of the market; the political and social revolutions of the two succeeding centuries—all have formed and shaped a civilization which has only begun to develop its full potential.

This adventure of Western man cannot but arouse admiration. Surely the effort of humanity to escape from primitive animality, to master nature through an understanding of its laws, to civilize itself by learning to understand itself, to bring more light, happiness and beauty into the world, to surmount the challenges which beset it on every side, to look inward for the improvement of the human condition provides a vision far more inspiring than that of a fallen humanity in which a chosen few owe their salvation solely to grace from on high.

Western civilization is the outcome of a mentality which insists on freeing itself from taboos, interdicts, and ancestral customs devoid of social utility; which forces itself to understand the surrounding world so that it may master it by its own laws; which ceaselessly strives to improve the conditions of life so that existence may be worth living for the greatest possible number; but which always insists that progress can come only through processes which respect the dignity of the individual.

This civilization is not restricted to particular geographical or political groups. The West exists wherever the names of Thales, Hippocrates, Euclid, Archimedes, Cicero, Gaius, Leonardo, Bacon, Galileo, Descartes, Locke, Montesquieu, Voltaire, Beccaria, Adam Smith, Hamilton and Jefferson are known and their messages understood. Wherever the rights of man and the procedures which safeguard them prevail, wherever the rules of scientific inquiry are followed, wherever freedom of thought and speech are respected, there is the West. A state may once have belonged to the West, but if it is faithless to its principles, temporarily or permanently, it loses the right to call itself Western. Two-thirds of the peoples of the world believe they have been denied what the West regards as a better way of life. It is still an open question whether this sense of denial is spontaneous or induced. A people may refuse to make the prolonged efforts which produced this thing we call Western society; they have a perfect right to prefer the patriarchal simplicity of biblical times. What the West calls progress may appear to some men to be a restlessness devoid of meaning. We have no right to impose upon them our values and our standards of conduct. But everyone has the duty to maintain the conditions needed for peaceful coexistence until they are willing to enter into effective cooperation. Blind xenophobia and fanatical patriotism are diseases fatal to man and society alike.

Western civilization need not be ashamed of having tried to improve the human lot by combating misery, violence and disdain for the individual. In stealing fire from heaven, Prometheus, the very embodiment of the West, seems to have inspired the sons of Greece with a creative energy which gave them the courage to defy the prohibitions of the jealous gods, even at the cost of life itself. The Greek dramatist Aeschylus wrote a sequel to his play *Prometheus Bound* (we now possess only a fragment of it, but it was called *Prometheus Unbound*), in which Hercules rescues Prometheus, who then leads men to a golden age of peace. Let us hope our Promethean civilization may be saved from its vultures, and that it may penetrate into the hearts and spirits of all the human families whose destinies are linked together on this tiny planet.

NOTES

CHAPTER I

1. In *Prometheus Bound*, the only part of a trilogy which has survived, Aeschylus, the Athenian tragic poet (525–456 B.C.), has Prometheus describe the miseries of mankind until "I gave them understanding and the power to think. . . . I opened for them the secret treasures of earth. . . . All human industry and arts," he boasted, "came from me" (456-506).

2. Lucretius, *De rerum natura*, I, 62-67.

3. Hermannus Diels, *Doxographi Graeei* (Berlin, 1829), 107.

4. Proclus, *Commentary on the First Book of Euclid*, I, 1.

5. For Ahmose, a circle is a *ring* and a point is located within, on, or outside of this ring; for a Greek geometrician, a circle is the geometric *locus of points* equidistant from a given point, and any point on the same plane as the circle is smaller, equal to, or greater in distance from that given point than the circle's radius. For Ahmose, a triangle whose sides are multiples of the numbers 3, 4 and 5 will include a right angle; for the Greek geometricians the intuitive property of forming a right angle is expressed by a mathematical relationship among the numbers representing the three sides, namely, the square of one of the numbers is equal to the sum of the squares of the other two. The property of the "sacred" triangle 3–4–5, which gave the surveyors of the Nile Valley a practical means for constructing an exact perpendicular, is merely one case of the theory of Pythagoras which permitted the complete geometric solution, by means of easy constructions derived from it, of what the

Greeks called plane geometry and which we express in equations of the second degree.

6. Greek progress in this discipline was prodigious. The discovery of incommensurables, the theory of proportions, and the method of exhaustion of Eudoxus, as developed by Archimedes; the notion of curvilinear space applied by Euclid to the theory of optics; the trigonometric relationships used by Aristarchus of Samos and by Hipparchus; the study of conic sections by Appollonius of Perga, including the use of the parabola to describe the path of projectiles of Greek artillery and the hyperbole of the shadow case on sun dials; the procedure of integration based on the comparative study of static moments of two objects as applied by Archimedes; the discovery of acceptable approximations for *pi* and other irrational numbers necessary for the solution of such practical problems as maps and the hydraulic wheel; geometric algebra culminating in the algebra of Diophantus—these were among the highest realizations of Greek geometricians.

7. Hesiod, *Theogony*, 116-32.

8. In the *Iliad* Homer describes the earth as a flat disc, surrounded by the river Ocean, son of the Sky and Earth. The Sky is a bell-shaped cover over which the Sun and the Moon ride on chariots carried by clouds. At night the Sun returns to the east, following along the river Ocean and just a little bit below the line of the horizon.

9. Plato, *Laws*, X, 889B.

10. *Ibid.*, 889C.

11. "Nothing," declared Plato in *The Republic*, "is better than to admire the beauty and the order of the complicated and varied movements afforded to us by the sky; but the beauty of movements visible to the senses is very much inferior to that of the real movements. These real movements are the real speed and the real slowness in true number and true figures, both in relation to one another and as vehicles of the things they carry and contain. These can be apprehended only by reason and thought, but not by sight" (VII, 529).

12. He reached this extraordinarily precise figure by measuring the angle made by the sun's rays at Alexandria when it cast no shadow at Syrene, a place believed to be on the same meridian and 500 stades distant.

13. Thus, in the only treatise on architecture which has come down to us from antiquity (Vitruvius, *On Architecture*), we find this revealing

passage. "Proportion . . . is attained when the details of the work are of a height suitable to their breadth, or a breadth suitable to their length; in short when everything has a symmetrical correspondence" (I. 2. 4). Edited from Harlean Ms. 2767 and translated into English by Frank Granger (Cambridge, Mass., 1931).

Symmetry, as the Greeks understood the term and as the etymology of the word indicates, is the key to the aesthetics of antiquity. Treatises on architecture in Greek and Latin which cite Vitruvius are almost all entitled *Treatises on Symmetry.* The Doryphore of Polyclitus, now at the Naples Museum, the Temple of the Concorde at Agrigente, the vault of St. Sophia at Byzantium, a Greek vase, a Doric column, an entablature, an architrave, the minutest decorative design—all obey rules of proportion so rigorously that Vignole, the master of modern architecture, after carefully measuring the proportions of the most beautiful buildings of ancient Rome, found among them a harmony of parts so exact that one could deduce exactly the measurements of all the parts from the tiniest molding, just as Cuvier could reconstruct antediluvian species from a simple molar.

CHAPTER II

1. Herodotus, *History,* Bk. III, 80.

2. Aristotle, *Politics,* 6. 5, 6 (1317a).

3. Thucydides, *History,* II, 37.

4. Aeschylus, *The Persians* (Medicean text), nos. 402-4.

5. Epictetus, *Discourses,* III, 2 and I, 7.

6. *The Republic,* 443D-E.

7. An ancient document (the papyrus of Rhind) describes the methods land surveyors of the Nile Valley used in their work. The significant thing about this papyrus is that the author, writing fifteen centuries before our era, declares emphatically that it is an identical copy of a manuscript written a century earlier in the reign of King Amenemhat! The Egyptian practice of medicine, if we may believe the account given by Diodorus of Sicily, slavishly followed "written law which was composed in ancient times by many famous physicians. If they followed the rules . . . as found in the sacred books and yet are unable to save their patient, they are exonerated and go unpunished; but if they go contrary to the prescriptions of the law in any respect, they undergo

trial and can be condemned to death, the lawgivers believing that few physicians of the present could be wiser than the treatment which had been closely followed for so long a time and which had originally been prescribed by the ablest practitioners of the art" (Diodorus of Sicily, *History*, I, 82).

This same stagnation prevailed for Sumer and its cuneiform writing. Beginning with 2,000 symbols, the number was reduced to 800 by 3000 B.C. and to 600 five hundred years later. Even so, mastery of the art of writing required long years of study. This was a task that fell to the priests and scribes trained in the temple schools. As in Egypt they copied with patient exactitudes old texts from long-forgotten times. When learning is chained to a writing which, because of the difficulty of mastering it, necessarily becomes the prerogative of a tiny caste of scribes, accepted knowledge becomes fixed and rigid.

8. Quoted by Kathleen Freeman, *Ancilla to the Pre-Socratic Philosophers* (Cambridge, Mass., 1948), p. 22.

9. Hermannus Diels, *Fragmente der Vorsokratiker*, 2 vols. (Berlin, 1903-7), I, 11, 15 and 16.

10. Pindar, *Olympians*, I, 28-33.

11. Diels, *op. cit.,* 55.

12. Julian, *Oeuvres complètes,* ed. E. Talbot (Paris, 1863), p. 336.

13. Ernest Renan, *History of the People of Israel* (Boston, 1888), p. vii.

CHAPTER III

1. Rudolph von Ihering, *L'esprit du droit romain,* 3 vols., (French trans., 1887), III, pp. 157-58.

2. Cicero, *De re publica,* III. 22.

3. Vergil, *Aeneid,* VI, 251-53.

4. Tacitus, *Annals,* XI, 24. 1.

5. Aelius Aristides, *Panegyric of Marcus Aurelius,* ed. Dindorf, *Oeuvres,* XIV, 16.

6. Rutilius Namatiamus, cited by Gaston Boismier, *La fin du paganism,*
II, 199.

7. Von Ihering, *op. cit.,* I, pp. 2 and 8.

8. The same aspiration lived again in Dante's *Universal Monarchy,* in
Pierre Dubois's *Christian Republic,* in Sully's *Great Design,* in Comen-
ius's *Universal Awakening,* in William Penn's *International Diet,* in the
Abbé de Saint-Pierre's *Perpetual Peace,* in St. Simon's *Program for a
European Society,* in Victor Hugo's call for a Peace Congress and a
United States of Europe, in the League of Nations, in the United Na-
tions, and in the "one world" extolled by Bertrand Russell.

9. Winston Churchill, *A History of the English-Speaking Peoples,* vol. 1:
The Birth of Britain (New York, 1966), pp. 15-16.

CHAPTER IV

1. Robert Oppenheimer found it amazing that the scientific revolution
did not occur at thi. time. "The Greeks made discoveries without which
our world would not be what it is: accurate standards, the ideas of
proof, logical necessity and implication. Without these ideas, science is
practically impossible. . . . They had . . . a very high degree of technical
refinement. They were able to make very subtle and complicated instruments, and yet they . . . seldom referred to them in their writings"
("Science et Culture," *Les Études philosophiques,* no. 4 [1964], p. 522).

2. Aristotle, *Politics,* I, 4, 1253b.

3. On slavery in antiquity: H. Wallon, *Histoire de l'esclavage dans
l'Antiquité,* 2nd ed., 3 vols. (Paris, 1879); W. L. Westermann, *The Slave
System of Greek and Roman Antiquity* (Philadelphia, 1955); A. Aymard,
"Stagnation, technique et esclavage" (L. H. Parias, *Histoire générale du
travail,* I [Paris, 1962], pp. 371-77).

4. Plutarch, *Lives:* Marcellus, XVII, 4.

5. Aristotle, *Politics,* I, 2, 1252a.

6. *Ibid.,* I, 4, 1253b.

7. *Ibid.*

8. Gaston Bossier, *La réligion romaine* (Paris, 1909), II, p. 359.

9. Quintilian, *De institutione oratorias*, XII, 11.

10. Seneca (d. 65 A.D.) appears to have come close to the idea of progress, but only with respect to knowledge. "A time will come when what is concealed today will be revealed to future generations. . . . The future will know things we now do not know, and will be astonished that we have ignored what it knows. Nature doesn't . . . offer herself for all to see; she hides and secrets herself in the deepest recesses; our century discovered part of her and other centuries will discover other parts" (*Questiones naturales,* vii). It was from Seneca's inspiration that the idea of progress (rejected by Christianity) was to reappear in the Middle Ages in the person of Roger Bacon, and then in the Renaissance in the Italian humanist Pico della Mirandola (d. 1494), and a century later in the French essayist Montaigne, an avid reader of Seneca.

11. Lucretius, *De rerum natura*, V, 1035.

12. Plutarch, *Lives:* Tiberius Gracchus, IX.

13. Cited by René Pichon, *Histoire de la litterature latine* (Paris, 1898), p. 167.

CHAPTER V

1. I Corinthians 7:20-22 (RSV).

2. Ephesians 6:9 (RSV).

3. Cited by A. Aymard (L. H. Parias, *Histoire générale du travail*), p. 374.

4. Galatians 3:28 (RSV).

5. The Theodosian Code (438) stipulated that the distinguished exercise of a trade could lead to the dignity of a Count of the first order.

6. II Thessalonians 3:10 (RSV).

7. Rule no. 48, cited in *Western Asceticism*, Library of Christian Classics, Vol. XII (Philadelphia, 1958), pp. 290 ff.

8. Maricourt, known for his theory of magnetism, was a precursor of Leonardo da Vinci. Roger Bacon hailed him as the master of experimentation "who knows . . . the laws of nature, medicine, alchemy, all

things of heaven and earth" (Roger Bacon, *Opus tertium,* ed. Brewer [London, 1859], chap. 13).

CHAPTER VI

1. Politian, *Opera* (Lyons, 1533), III, 64.

2. His *Theologica Platonica* was designed to "deliver religion from its abominable ignorance." With the aid of subtle exegesis of texts, relying on a fourfold interpretation (literal, allegorical, topological and anagogical), Ficino made over into Fathers of the Church such pagan writers and religious leaders as Confucius, Zoroaster, Orpheus, the Cabalists, Parmenides, etc.

3. Ficino, *Opera* (Bale, 1576), p. 944.

4. André of Perusia, cited by Paul Herman, *L'Homme à la découverte du Monde* (Paris, 1954), p. 453.

CHAPTER VII

1. Leonardo da Vinci, *Treatise on Painting,* a lost book from the Codex Leicester by Carlo Pedritti, foreword by Sir Kenneth Clark (Berkeley, 1961), p. 1.

2. Leonardo da Vinci, *Manuscrit de l'Institut de France,* G.7.

3. Leonardo da Vinci, *Codice Atlantico,* 76r.a.

4. *Ibid..* 117, 4.b.

5. *Ibid.,* 154, r.c.

6. From *The Notebooks of Leonardo da Vinci,* 2 vols., arranged, rendered into English, and introduced by E. McCurdy (New York, 1938), I, p. 27.

7. Leonardo da Vinci, *Manuscrit de l'Institut de France,* G.8r.

8. Bacon's views as summarized here will be found in book 2, chapter 1, of his *Novum organum.* An English translation of the *Novum organum*

appears in vol. 30 of *The Great Books of the Western World,* ed. Robert Hutchins (Chicago, 1952), pp. 32 ff.

9. *Ibid.,* p. 137.

10. *Oeuvres du Chancelier Bacon,* trans. Bucon (Paris: Le Panthéon litteraire, 1938), p. 596.

11. René Descartes, *Discourse on Method,* VI.

12. F. S. Mason, *Histoire des sciences* (Paris, 1956).

CHAPTER VIII

1. I Corinthians 3:19 (RSV).

2. *The Writings of Tertullian,* trans. Peter Holmes (Edinburgh, 1870), p. 9.

3. I Corinthians 8:1 (RSV).

4. Augustine, *Soliloquies,* I:2.

5. Pierre Duhem, "Le système du monde," in *Histoire des doctrines cosmologiques de Platon à Copernic,* 8 vols. (Paris, 1913-54), III, 11, and II, 393.

6. *Pensées de M. Pascal sur la religion et sur quelques autres sujets,* ed. Brunschvig (Paris, 1943), p. 361. In 1966 Penguin published an English translation of the *Pensées* with an introduction by A. J. Krailsheimer.

7. "Symbole de Saint Athanase," *La Foi catholique* (Paris, 1961), p. 30.

8. Augustine, *Commentary on Genesis,* III, 135; *City of God,* XVI, 9.

9. A. G. Little, ed., *Roger Bacon, Essays* (Oxford, 1914), p. 26.

10. II Corinthians 12:2.

11. Paolo Sarpi, *Istoria del Consilio Tridentino,* II, 91.

12. Osiander, *De revolutionibus orbium coelestium,* ed. Nuremberg (1543), feuillet 1.

13. C. F. Kepler, *Joannis Kepleri astronomi opera omnia* (Frankfurt am Main, 1858–71), III, 154.

14. *Le Opera di Galileo Galilei* (Florence, 1842–50), II, 24 ff.

15. Giorgio Santillana, *Le procès de Galilée* (Paris, 1955), p. 229.

16. See K. von Gebler, *Die Akten der galileischen Processes nach der vatikanischen Handschrift herausgegeben* (Stuttgart, n.d.), pp. 11 ff.

17. Galilée, *Dialogues et lettres choisies* (Paris, 1967), p. 430.

18. Ernest Renan, *Oeuvres complètes* (Paris, 1955), VII, p. 990.

19. Santillana, *op. cit.*, p. 404. The book and a copy of the *Letter to the Grand Duchess* were sent secretly to Mathias Bernegger, a friend of Kepler, by Diodeli, a lawyer and member of the Parliament of Paris. Bernegger prepared a Latin translation of the *Dialogue* (1637). A year earlier he had published in Italian and in Latin the *Letter.* On June 26, 1636, Galileo could announce with joy this publication to Father Fulgencio Micanzio at Venice, and express the hope that copies could be smuggled into Italy "for the confusion of our enemies." He entrusted the manuscript of his new work, *Dialogue on Two New Sciences,* to the Comte de Noailles, French Ambassador to Rome, who was authorized by the Inquisition to visit him. The count had the work secretly printed in Holland.

CHAPTER IX

1. Lucretius, *De natura rerum,* II, 1144 ff.

2. Horace, *Ode II.*

3. Quoted in *Collections des grands écrivains: Oeuvres,* vol. II (Paris, 1908), p. 129.

4. *Oeuvres de Turgot* (Paris, 1913–20), vol. I, 71.

5. *Oeuvres complètes de Buffon,* 6 vols. (Paris, 1839–41). The passage appears in the seventh and last of his "Époques de la nature."

6. Condorcet, *Esquisse d'un tableau historique du progres de l'esprit humain,* Dixième Époque, to be found in *Oeuvres de Condorcet,* ed. A. C. O'Conner and M. F. Arago (Paris, 1847–49).

7. This and the immediately following citations are from Robert Mauzi, *L'Idée du bonheur dans les lettres et la pensée française* au XVIII^{em} siècle (Paris, 1966), pp. 80 ff.

8. *Oeuvres choisies de Vico,* trans. Jules Michelet (Paris, 1855), vol. I, p. 396.

9. Jules Michelet, *Introduction à l'histoire universelle* (Paris, 1831), p. 9.

CHAPTER X

1. Cicero, *De officiis,* XLII.

2. Cited by J. Le Goff, *Marchands et banquiers du moyne age* (Paris, 1956), pp. 80-82.

3. Deuteronomy 23:19 (RSV).

4. Luke 6: 34-35 (RSV).

5. Cited by Le Goff, *op. cit.,* p. 72.

6. Richard Baxter, *A Christian Directory* (London, 1678), I, chap. X, tit. 8, dist. 9.

7. Cited by Max Weber, *Archiv. f. Sozialwirtschaft u. Socialpolitik,* vol. III, p. 86.

8. Robert Southey, *Life of Wesley* (2nd ed.; London, 1825), vol. II, p. 308. It is worth noting that as late as the mid-fifties of this century not a single Catholic canton in Switzerland had a per capita income as high as the poorest Protestant canton.

9. Poor Richard, *The Almanac for the Years 1733–1758,* ed. Richard Saunders (New York, 1964), pp. 278-85.

CHAPTER XI

1. Matthew 19:24 (RSV).

2. Adam Smith, *An Inquiry into the Nature and Causes of the Wealth of Nations,* Everyman's Library Edition (London, 1910). Smith's dis-

cussion of mercantilism (Bk. IV, *passim*) exerted an enormous influence on his contemporaries.

3. One of the first writers to emphasize the close relationship between free trade and war was Eméric Crucé. In the *Nouveau Cynée* (1623) he called free trade "a universal police," capable of ensuring a "peace which gives to each man what he deserves, privilege to the citizen, hospitality to the stranger, and to everyone equally freedom of movement and negotiation."

4. Mercier de la Rivière, *L'heureuse nation ou relations du gouvernement des féliciens* (Paris, 1792), vol. I, pp. 242-43.

5. Smith, *op. cit.*, I, chap. I, p. 5.

6. *Ibid.*, I, chap. 2, p. 13.

7. *Ibid.*, I, chap. 8, p. 70.

8. *Ibid.*, I, p. 78.

9. Robert Heilbroner, *The Worldly Philosophers: The Lives, Times and Ideas of the Great Economic Thinkers* (New York, 1953), p. 31.

10. Smith, *op. cit.*, I, chap. 8, p. 73.

11. Quoted by Heilbroner, *op. cit.*, p. 69.

12. Smith, *op. cit.*, IV, chap. 2, p. 400.

13. J. B. Say, *Oeuvres diverses,* p. 545.

CHAPTER XII

1. Cited by Paul Mantoux, *The Industrial Revolution in the 18th Century: An Outline of the Beginnings of the Modern Factory System in England* (New York, 1961), p. 387.

2. Whether these operations are accomplished by mechanical, hydraulic or electromagnetic connections, or by human nervous cells, circuits and vacuum tubes or by human sensory cells, nerves and synapses, it is still true that their mechanisms, or speaking more precisely, the structure of their mechanisms, are identical. In this connection see Norbert

Wiener, *Cybernetics or Control and Communication in the Animal and
the Machine* (2nd ed.; Cambridge, Mass., 1965).

3. Norbert Wiener, *Cybernetics and Society: The Human Use of
Human Beings* (Boston, 1950); Louis Couffignal, *Les Machines à penser*
(Paris, 1952).

CHAPTER XIII

1. Julius Caesar claimed descent from Venus because he realized that
in the eyes of the multitude this gave him the clearest possible title to
be the master of the city and the world. Mark Antony presented himself to the masses in the East as the reincarnation of Dionysus. Elagabalus claimed descent from the Syrian Baal.

2. Montesquieu, *The Spirit of the Laws*, trans. T. Nugent; ed. F. Neu-
man. Hafner Library of Classics (New York, 1949), Bk. IX, chap. 4.

3. *World Book Encyclopedia*, Magna Carta, vol. XII, p. 48.

4. Sophocles's *Antigone* invoked the "unwritten law" as superior to all
man-made laws. Socrates called it divine. Aristotle contrasted written
and specific laws with the common law, which is eternal and necessary.
Another idea was closely associated with this—that of a "social contract,"
a form of written law, inferior to natural law, which results from agreement among members of a single community. Demosthenes (d. 322 B.C.)
defined law as "a contract which binds all the citizens and which all
the inhabitants of the city must obey" (*Contra Aristogiton*, I, 16). These
ideas were picked up by Cicero, by the early Church Fathers and by
later theorists of natural right.

5. Blackstone, *Commentaries*, ed. Chitty (New York, 1884), I, 1, p. 129.

6. Flammermont, *Remonstrances*, III, p. 279.

7. The French mind, classical and Cartesian, excels in formulating
abstract principles, which it tends to regard as good for all times and
all peoples. Those announced in the Declaration of the Rights of
Man and Citizen possessed such self-evident and universal truths that
Anarcharsis Cloots, speaking in the name of the delegates from many
lands who had come to pay homage to the National Assembly, voiced
their sentiments by declaring, "When I look at a world map, it seems
to me that all other countries have disappeared; my eyes see only
France, the regenerator of peoples everywhere" (*Moniteur*, reimpres-

sion, XIII, p. 661). And still today, like the trumpet of Jericho blowing down the walls of the world's Bastilles, the "immortal principles of 1789" symbolize the longings of the disinherited for more justice, well-being and liberty.

CHAPTER XIV

1. Deuteronomy 13:6-9 (RSV).

2. Elagabalus (d. 222) undertook to combine all cults including those of the Jews, the Samaritans and the Christians, by placing them under the supremacy of the sun-god Baal. Alexander Severus (d. 235) placed in his private chapel the busts of Apollonius, Christ, Abraham, Orpheus, Alexander the Great and others.

3. Tertullian, *Apology*, C. XXIV.

4. Deuteronomy 17:12 (RSV).

5. Cited by Constant Martha, *Études sur l'antiquité* (Paris, 1883), p. 257.

6. A. Baudrillart, *L'Église catholique, la renaissance, le protestantisme* (Paris, 1904), p. 322.

7. Condorcet, *Oeuvres de Condorcet*, ed. A. C. O'Connor and M. F. Arago, 6em Epoque.

8. Castalion anticipated Descartes in calling "doubt" the first step in the pursuit of truth.

9. John Locke, *A Letter Concerning Toleration*, vol. VI in *The Works of John Locke* (11th ed.; London, 1812), p. 52.

10. Voltaire's *Treatise on Toleration* appeared in 1783, Lessing's *Nathan the Wise* in 1779. Also important were Schiller's *Don Carlos* and Goethe's *Egmond*, both appearing in 1787.

11. Letter of November 19, 1785.

12. John Milton, *Areopagitica* (London, 1819), p. 116.

13. Malesherbes, *Memoires sur la liberté* (Paris, 1809), p. 57.

14. Diderot, *Sur la liberté de la presse* (Paris, 1964), p. 81.

15. Victor Hugo, "Actes et paroles," *Oeuvres complètes* (Paris, 1880–83), vol. I, p. 415.

CHAPTER XV

1. Cited by Jacques and Robert Lacour-Gayet, *De Platon à la Terreur* (Paris, 1948), p. 198.

2. William Roepke, *The Social Crisis of Our Time* (Chicago, 1950), p. 46.

3. Jules Michelet, *Le Peuple* (Paris, 1846), p. 84.

4. François R. Chateaubriand, "L'Avenir du Monde," *Revue des Deux Mondes* (April, 1934).

5. Lionel Robbins, *The Theory of Economic Policy in English Classical Political Economy* (London, 1952).

6. See André Siegfried, *Tableaux des États-Unis* (Paris, 1954), chap. 19; F. L. Allen, *The Big Chance* (New York, 1952); R. W. Davenport, *U. S. A.: The Permanent Revolution* (New York, 1952).

CHAPTER XVI

1. Counting and the use of a decimal system with a blank space for zero appeared by the first century B.C. Under the Sungs (960–1276) and the Yuans (1280–1368), the Chinese were the first to solve algebraic equations.

2. Joseph Needham, "Grandeur et faibless de la tradition scientifique chinoise," *La Pensée*, No. 111 (October, 1963), p. 7. See also his *Science and Civilization in China* (Cambridge, Eng., 1954–65), vol. III, pp. 159 ff.

3. For the entire text see F. White, *China and the Foreign Powers* (London, 1937).

4. Sylvain Lévy, *L'Inde et le monde* (Paris, 1952), pp. 9-10.

5. In opening a UNESCO-sponsored discussion at New Delhi in December 1951 between scholars from the East and the West, his Excellency Maulanu Abdul Kalam Azad, Indian Minister of Education,

recognized the relative insensibility of Indian people to human suffering, "since suffering is considered as a pure illusion," and admitted that "oriental thought, being preoccupied with individual salvation, has sometimes given too little attention to social welfare and progress" (Maulanu Azad, *Humanism et Education en Orient et en Occident* [UNESCO, 1953], p. 40). The Swami Siddheswarannanda added, in answer to those who have criticized the West for its excessive preoccupation with technological matters, for its devotion to materalism and seeming disregard for man's higher aspirations: "When tens of thousands of human beings in the East have nothing to eat, to speak of humanism and of the ideal man is nothing but a caricature. What is needed are effective measures for abolishing ignorance, famine and sickness" (*ibid.*, p. 228). And Arthur Koestler returned from his pilgrimage to India completely disillusioned, finding there no spiritual cure for the ills besetting Western civilization (*The Lotus and the Robot* [New York, 1961]).

6. Marmoun maintained at his own expense a group of translators, headed by Al-Khwarizmi, who wrote an algebra inspired by Brahmaputra (600 B.C.) and drew up trigonometric tables, making use of the sines, and astronomical tables based upon the findings of Ptolemy and Brahmaputra. Al-Khwarizmi was followed by Tabit ibn Morra, who translated *The Almagest* of Ptolemy and devoted himself to the solution of equations cf the third degree. In the tenth century it was still at Baghdad that the celebrated mathematician Albatenius and the great astronomer Aboul-Wafa carried on their studies. It was at Baghdad that the Persian doctor Al-Razi pursued his medical studies in the late ninth century and published his thirty-volume medical encyclopedia, bringing together all the known medical knowledge since the time of Hippocrates.

CHAPTER XVII

1. Quoted by William Roepke, *A Humane Economy: The Social Framework of a Free Market* (Chicago, 1960), Foreword, opening paragraph.

2. Claude Adrien Helvetius, *De l'homme* (Paris, 1959), sect. IV, chap. 2.

3. Quoted by Emile Faquet, *Discussions politiques* (Paris, n.d.), p. 318.

4. "Supplement au voyage de Bougainville," *Oeuvres,* ed. Asiegat and Tourneux (Paris, n.d.), vol. II, 240-41.

5. Helvetius, *De l'esprit,* discour II, chap. 15.

6. Condorcet, *Oeuvres de Condorcet,* ed. A. C. O'Connor and M. F. Arago, 378.

7. Cited by René Pichon, *Histoire de la litterature latine* (Paris, 1898), p. 578.

8. Henri Bergson, *The Two Sources of Morality and Religion* (Garden City, 1954), p. 290.

9. Alexis de Tocqueville, *Democracy in America* (New York, 1966), vol. II, part 5, chap. 6.

10. Friedrich Engels, *Anti-Duhring* (Moscow, 1962), p. 249.

INDEX

Abbasids, 86, 177
Academies, 73
Acton, Lord, 130
Aeschylus, 199, 201, 203
Ahmose, 4, 201
Anarchy, 129, 138
Alembert, Jean le Rond d', 149, 195
Alexander Severus (Emperor), 213
Alexandria, school of, 65
Almohades, 178
ama nescire, 63, 75, 193
Anaximander, 7
Anaximenes, 8
Apollonius of Pergama, 20, 65, 195, 202
Aquinas, Thomas, 78, 97
"Arabian Miracle," 177-79, 184
Arago, M. F., 209
Archimedes, 10, 20, 35, 65, 66, 185, 183, 195, 198, 202
Aretino, 62
Aristarchus, 11, 81, 202
Aristides, Aelius, 30, 204
Aristocracy, 14, 127
Aristotle, 4, 11, 21, 34, 36, 52, 59, 66, 71, 76, 77, 81, 82, 85, 87, 95, 130, 166, 203, 205, 212

Arkwright, Richard, 113, 118
Art, 12
Asclepiades, 3
Athanasian Creed, 145, 208
Atheism, 62
Augustine (Saint), 75, 76, 193, 208
Augustus (Emperor), 41
Aymard, A., 206
Azad, Maulanu Abdul Kalam, 214

Babeuf, François Noël, 161
Bacon, Francis, 67, 69-70, 207, 208
Bacon, Roger, 52, 76, 198, 207, 208
Bargaining, collective, 164
Barre, de la, 149
Baudrillart, Alfred, 213
Baxter, Richard, 102, 210
Bayle, Pierre, 148
Beccaria, Caesar Bonasana, 198
Bell, Alexander Graham, 119
Benedetti, 66
Bentham, Jeremy, 115
Bergson, Henri Louis, 186, 216
Bernegger, 209
Berthollet, Claude Louis, 119
Bessemer, Henry, 119
Bicameralism, 130, 136
Blackstone, William, 135, 212

Bodin, Jean, 195
Bossuet, Jacques Bénigne, 93
Botticelli, Sandro, 56
Boulton, Matthew, 118
Boyle, Robert, 117
Brahmaputra, 215
Brunelleschi, Filippo, 60
Bruno, Giordano, 71
Buddhism, 174
Buffon, Comte de, 91, 209

Cabet, Etienne, 161
Caesar, Julius, 29, 41, 212
Calas, Jean, 149
Calixtus I (Pope), ?
Callippus, 10
Calvin, John, 77, 84, 99, 148
Calvinism, 100
Capitalism, 54, 95, 97, 102, 105, 108, 165-69
Carnot, Sadi, 119
Castalion, Sébastien, 148, 213
Catullus, 29
Cellini, Benevenuto, 62
Censorship, 81, 151
Charity and self-interest, 114-16
Chateaubriand, François René de, 159
Chien Lung (Emperor), 173
Chrysoloras, Manuel, 59
Chrysostom, John (Saint), 45
Churchill, Sir Winston, 31, 205
Cicero, Marcus Tullius, 27, 29, 95, 130, 140, 198, 204, 210, 212
Cincinnatus, 41
Civilization, 2, 21, 191, 197; African, 89; Chinese, 171-74; Eastern, 21, 171; medieval, 56. See also Mentality and civilization —Western, 2, 21, 65, 89, 154, 159, 170, 184, 191, 197; Christianity's contribution to, 184, 197; Greek contribution to, 2, 25, 27, 62, 184, 193; Roman contribution to, 27-28, 62
Clark, Colin, 90, 124

Claudius I (Emperor), 29
Cloots, Anarcharsis, 212
Colbert, Jean Baptiste, 73, 109, 156
Columbus, Christopher, 63
Comte, Auguste, 93
Condorcet, Marquis de, 91, 92, 93, 147, 195, 209, 213, 216
Confucianism, 172-73, 194
Confucius, 172-73, 207
Conscience, right of, 127
Constitutionalism, 130
Constitutions: American, 135-37, 150, 153; French, 139-140
Contract, 108; social, 135, 138, 212
Copernicus, Nicolaus, 64, 69, 74, 81, 83, 84
Corporations, medieval, 155
Counter-Reformation, 62, 80
Crassus, M. Licinius, 41
Crèvecoeur, Saint-Jean de, 92
Crompton, Samuel, 118
Custom, 129
Cybernetics, 122-24
Cynics, 3, 45

Dante Alighieri, 57, 60, 78, 88, 205
Declaration of Independence, 92, 135
Declaration of Rights of Man and Citizen, 137, 150, 153, 158, 212
Democracy, 13, 14, 15, 20, 128, 133, 135
Democritus, 22
Demosthenes, 58, 59, 212
Descartes, René, 66, 67, 72, 74, 198, 208
Diderot, Denis, 89, 149, 152, 213
Diophantus, 202
Disraeli, Benjamin, 159
Djilas, Milovan, 163
Dubois, Pierre, 205
Duhem, Pierre, 75, 208

Edict of Nantes, 149
Education and perfectibility of man, 181-82

Elagabalus (Emperor), 213
Encyclopédie, 152
Engels, Friedrich, 190, 216
Enlightenment, 180-83
Epictetus, 203
Epicurus, 2
Ethics, 18, 95, 103
Euclid, 6, 171, 195, 198, 202
Eudoxus of Cnidus, 3
Eudoxus of Rhodes, 21, 202

Faith, and truth, 83
Faquet, Emile, 215
Fatimids, 177
Ficino, Marsilio, 59, 207
Ford, Henry, 125, 164, 165
Fourier, Charles, 161
Franklin, Benjamin, 104-05, 125
Free Trade, 109, 110
Frederick II, 178
Fugger family, 54, 63

Gaius, 198
Galen, 33, 76, 177
Galilei, Galileo, 10, 52, 64, 66, 70-71, 80-84, 86, 89, 151, 185, 198, 209
Gandhi, Mohandras Karamchand, 125
Gebler, K. von, 209
Goethe, Johann Wolfgang von, 213
Gozzoli, Benozzo, 59
Gracchus, Tiberius, 40
Grand Duchess of Tuscany, 82-83
Gratian, 97
Grossteste, Robert, 52

habeas corpus, 130, 131
Hamilton, Alexander, 198
Happiness, 92, 135, 140, 190
Hargreaves, James, 118
Harmony, social, 114
Harun Al-Rashid, 177, 178
Hegel, George Wilhelm Friedrich, 93, 192
Heilbroner, Robert, 211

Helvetius, 181, 215
Heraclitus, 3
Herodotus, 3, 14, 203
Heron, 36, 195
Herschel, William, 89
Hesiod, 3, 7, 22, 202
Hinduism, 174
Hipparchus, 3, 11, 21, 33, 202
Hippocrates, 33, 177, 198, 215
Hobbes, Thomas, 135
Homer, 3, 22, 58, 59, 202
Honnecourt, Villard de, 49, 52
Horace, 42, 90, 209
Hugo, Victor, 154, 205. 214
Humanism, 56 f.
Hume, David, 114
Huss, John, 147
Hutcheson, Francis, 114
Huxley, Aldous, 196

Ibn-Khaldun, 179
Ihering, Rudolph von, 30, 204, 205
Industrial revolution. *See* Revolution
Inquisition, 76, 146, 151
Interest, 98, 102
Intolerance, 145-50, 181
Inventions: Chinese, 171; medieval, 48-51. *See also* Galilei Galileo; Vinci, Leonardo da; Revolution, industrial
"Invisible hand," 115
Islam, 85, 176, 178

Jacquard, J. M., 118
Jerome of Prague, 147
Judicial review, 134, 136, 139
Julian (Emperor), 23, 193, 204

Kay, John, 118
Kepler, Johannes, 64, 65, 82, 86, 89, 185, 208
Koestler, Arthur, 215

Labor, attitudes toward, 44, 46, 47, 95, 97, 100-05, 114, 184

Lacour-Gayet, Jacques Robert, 214
Lactantius, 63
"laissez-faire, laissez-passer," 110
Laplace, Pierre Simon, 195
Lassalle, Ferdinand, 159
Lavoisier, Antoine Laurent, 119
Law, 27, 28, 131, 155; canon, 98;
    civil, 27; French, 138; natural,
    26; Roman, 26, 176
Legitimacy, principle of, 129, 134
Le Goff, J., 210
Lessing, Gollhold Ephraim, 148,
    213
Lévy, Sylvain, 214
Lewis, Sinclair, 187
Liberty, 68, 134-35, 138, 142, 143,
    151, 153
libido sciendi, 75
Liebig, Justus von, 120
Lippmann, Walter, xvi
Little, A. G., 208
Locke, John, 28, 134, 135, 150, 198,
    213
Lollards, 158
Lorenzetti, Ambrogio, 54
Luceti, Fortuno, 85
Lucretius, 1, 29, 90, 201, 209
Luther, Martin, 82, 84, 100
Lutheranism, 100, 128

McCormick, Cyrus, 120
Machiavelli, Niccolà, 62
Magna Carta, 131, 135, 212
Malesherbes, Chrétien, 152
Malik al-Kamil, 178
Malthus, Thomas, 120, 159
Mansur, al-, 177
Mantoux, Paul, 211
Marcellinus, 146
Maricourt, Pierre de, 52, 216
Market economy, 18, 112, 126;
    accomplishments of, 165-69
Marmoun the Great, 177, 215
Marta, Constant, 213
Martin brothers, 119

Marx, Karl, 93, 115, 160, 161-63,
    191, 192
Marxism, 161-63, 185
Mason, F. S., 208
Mauzi, Robert, 210
Medicis, 58, 59, 60, 63, 99
Mentality and civilization, 1-2, 103,
    172-81
Mercantilism, 108-09
Messini, Gilbert de, 99
Michelet, Jules, 93, 158, 210, 214
Mill, John Stuart, 115
Milton, John, 151
Mohammed Abdoh, 180
Money, 17, 108
Montesquieu, Baron de, 92, 130,
    148, 195, 198, 212
Mortality, infant, 113, 168
Muslim Brotherhood, 180

Namatiamus, Rutilius, 205
Napoleon Bonaparte, 139, 140
Nationalism, 183
Nature, 6, 172; human, 72, 91, 180,
    181; law of, 110, 127
Needham, Joseph, 171, 214
Newcomen, Thomas, 117
Newton, Isaac, 64, 71, 86, 89, 185
Nietzsche, Friedrich, 93
Noailles, Comte de, 209

O'Conner, A. C., 209
Ommiades, 86, 176
Opinion vs. truth, 3
Oppenheimer, Robert, 205
Ortega y Gasset, José, 188
Orwell, George, 196
Osiander, Andreas, 81, 208
Owen, Robert, 161

Paleologus, John, 59
Pappus, 66, 194, 195
Parliament, 130, 132
Parliamentarism, 130, 139
Pascal, Blaise, 71, 74, 90, 208
Paul, Saint, 75, 78

Index [221]

Pax Romana, 31
Penn, William, 205
Perfectibility of man, 181-82
Pericles, 13
Physiocrats, 109, 110, 195
Pichon, René, 206, 216
Pico della Mirandola, Giovanni, 206
Pindar, 22, 204
Plato, 4, 8, 19, 24, 36, 58, 59, 77, 95, 202
Pliny the Elder, 41
Plotinus, 24
Plutarch, 205, 206
Politian, 207
Polo, Marco, 64
Polybius, 3, 58, 130
Pompey, 41
Pomponazzi, Pietro, 62
Pope, Alexander, 92
Popes: Clement VII, 99; Gregory XVI, 147; Innocent IV, 99; Leo X, 99; Paul III, 81; Paul IV, 80; Urban VIII, 84
Population, 167, 185
Porphyry, 193
Poverty, 97
Power, 130, 136
Proclus, 4, 201
Profits, 115, 163, 165
Progress: ideas of, 87-94, 173, 174, 175, 179, 180, 181, 183; risks of, 181-91
Promethius, myth of, 1, 116, 195, 198, 201
Property, 16, 134
Protestant ethic, 95-106
Proudhon, Pierre Joseph, 161
Ptolemy, 3, 10, 21, 32, 33, 215
Pythagoras, 4, 9, 10
Pythagoreans, 2, 8

Quesnay, François, 109

Raphael, Sanzio, 59
Reason (rationalism), xviii, 2, 6, 23, 176, 192

Reformation, 62, 80, 100, 101, 126, 147
Religion, 21, 22, 143, 144, 145, 146
Renaissance, 56-64, 126, 146, 195
Renan, Ernest, 25, 85, 204, 209
Representation, 130, 131
Revolution: agricultural, 120; American, 28, 137; economic, 106-16, 126; English, 132, 135; French, 28, 132, 149, 167, 183; industrial, 104, 117-25, 167, 185, 211; political, 126-41; scientific, 65-73, 126; social, 44, 126
Ricardo, David, 159
Rights: bills of, 131, 132, 137; divine, 129; natural, 134; origin of, 140, 141; property, 16, 134
Rights of man, 28, 129, 150, 153, 158, 198, 212
Rivière, Mercier de la, 110, 211
Robbins, Lionel, 213
Roepke, William, 157, 213, 215
Roland, Madame, 181
Rougier, Louis, xv, xvi
Rousseau, Jean Jacques, 90, 92, 135, 167

Sachs, Hans, 158
Saint Benedict, Rule of, 49
Saint-Just, Louis A. L. de, 92
Saint-Pierre, Abbé de, 205
Saint-Simon, Claude Henri de, 161, 205
Saladin, 178
Santillana, Giorgio, 209
Sarpi, Paolo, 80, 208
Savary, 117
Savonarola, Girolamo, 61
Say, Jean Baptiste, 116, 211
Schiller, Johann von, 213
Scholasticism, 52, 59, 77, 194
Science: Aristotle and, 77; China, 194; early Christianity and, 74, 75; purpose of, 69; theology and, 76
Self-interest and charity, 114-16

Servetus, 76
Siegfried, André, 123, 214
Sirven, 149
Skeptics, 3
Slavery, 33-46, 74, 157, 166, 167, 184, 190
Smith, Adam, 105, 109-16, 157, 195, 198, 210, 211
Socrates, 22, 24, 127, 212
Sophists, 23
Sophocles, 212
Southey, Robert, 210
Spencer, Herbert, 93
Spengler, Oswald, 93
State: deification of, 127; liberal concept of, 140
Status, 108
Stoics, 27, 45, 125, 144, 196
Strabo, 31
Strozzi, Palla, 58

Tacitus, 204
Taoism, 173, 194
Tartaglia, Nicollò, 10, 52
Terror, equilibrium of, 186, 189; reign of, 91, 139
Tertullian, 75, 145, 208, 213
Thales, 4, 7, 193, 198
Theodocian Code, 206
Theology and science, 76
Thucydides, 3, 58, 203
Tocqueville, Alexis de, 90, 136, 187, 216
Toleration, Act of, 150
Toynbee, Arnold, 1, 93
Truth: and faith, 83; and opinion, 3
Turgot, A. R. J., 91, 93, 109, 157, 209

Turks, 179

Ulpien, 27
Universe: early Christian views of, 88, 93; geographical discoveries, 63, 64; Greek views of, 6, 87, 88; oriental views of, 6, 64
Usury, 98
Utilitarianism, 105, 140

Varro, Marcus Terentius, 29
Vedas, 174
Vergil, 28, 29, 42, 204
Vesalius, 57, 76
Vespucci, Amerigo, 63
Vetruvius, 29
Vico, Giambattista, 93, 210
Vieta, 194
Vinci, Leonardo da, 10, 57, 60, 62, 66, 67-69, 198, 207
Vitruvius, 202-03
Voltaire, 92, 93, 148, 198, 213

Wages, 114
War, 189
Watt, James, 36, 117
Weber, Max, 93, 210
Wesley, John, 103
White, F., 214
Wiener, Norbert, 124, 211, 212

Xenophanes of Colophon, 22
Xenophon, 58, 95

Yoga, 174
Young, Arthur, 157

Zola, Emile, 159